Praise fo

MW00324003

A timely treasure that promotes personal and planetary healing. Each nugget of Dale's daily wisdom has the power to uplift, inspire and evoke action to move through change and challenge with heart-centered faith and gratitude.

— CHRISTINE BLACK CUMMINGS,
AUTHOR OF *BLACK-EYED SUSAN: A LOVE-CHILD FINDS HER FATHER AND HER SELF*

Dale Olansky's Fear to Faith: A Daily Guide to Finding Solace in an Uncertain World *provides practical information on how to deal with challenges we all face in our lives. She delves deep into spiritual principles and ancient wisdom. Her guidance and use of these principles, along with her powerful affirmations, are tantamount to a roadmap to living a successful life.*

— REV. LAURA SHACKELFORD,
ASSISTANT MINISTER, CENTER FOR SPIRITUAL LIVING PALM DESERT

At a time when many new authors are entering into the metaphysical teaching world, Dale's unique style allows the reader to apply her powerful teaching in a clear and concise process. Dale's writing style has a softness to it but is also direct, with steps to guide the motivated reader into making dramatic life changes.

— REV. DR. JOE HOOPER,
SPIRITUAL LEADER, CENTER FOR SPIRITUAL LIVING PALM DESERT

With compassion, tenderness and understanding born of candid introspection into life's personal challenges, Dale offers us insights of empowerment and courage. Her openness and receptivity to Divine Wisdom inspire us to take a leap of faith to confidently lead a fearless life, rooted in the all-embracing and protective love of Spirit. She daily lights a prayerful candle to dispel the darkness of our doubts in order to live in the light of our truth.

— VELMA HOPKINS

Dale Olansky offers a new voice that reflects her depth of knowledge, personal faith and years of spiritual counseling experience. Each daily lesson is your guide to building a life of faith, trust and your highest self. Her style is warm, bright and inviting. This book is timeless and will be your companion for many years.

— LINDA DIERKS,
AUTHOR OF *SPIN STRAW TO GOLD*

Fear to Faith

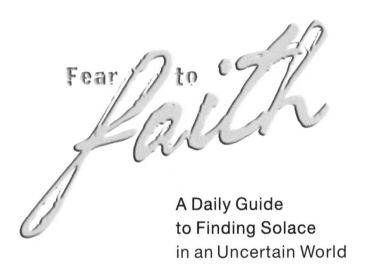

Fear to Faith

A Daily Guide to Finding Solace in an Uncertain World

Dale Olansky, RScP

FOREWORD BY REV. DR. MAXINE KAYE

PARK POINT PRESS
573 Park Point Drive
Golden, Colorado 80401-7042

Park Point Press
573 Park Point Drive
Golden, CO 80401-7402
720-496-1370

Printed in the United States of America
Published February 2019

Editor: Julie Mierau
Book design: Maria Robinson, Designs On You, LLC, Littleton CO

ISBN ebook: 978-0-917849-76-3
ISBN paperback: 978-0-917849-75-6

I dedicate this book to my mom,

Ilene Olansky,

who taught me to live

courageously

and never give in to fear.

FOREWORD

Dale Olansky is a woman of quiet power, authentically living her spiritual beliefs in ways that connect with others and assist them in navigating the challenging currents of current events. *Fear to Faith – A Daily Guide to Finding Solace in an Uncertain World* offers gentle and practical guidance to move us from confusion and concern into a deeper awareness of a wise and loving Presence upon which we may rely for sane solutions.

Knowing that neither becoming entrenched in fear nor descending into depression over appalling conditions in the world promotes emotional well-being, Dale offers short, effective, inspirational messages that bring us back to hopefulness and clarity of purpose. A busy person can invest just a few minutes in receiving serenity and encouragement and find the day unfolding with surprising grace and ease.

Dale's simple suggestions, clear reminders and uplifting ideas can raise a person's faith and provide tools to meet and succeed in either a personal or professional environment. She is both heavenly minded and down-to-earth, as she moves through her own life experiences and chooses, again and again, to continue shifting her consciousness from fear to faith. She is genuine in her approach, mindful of her audience and effective in communicating the promise of a better way to think, a healthier manner of believing and a more wholesome approach to life.

She helps lift the veil of ambiguity and assists in discovering a sound and sensible way to return to our innate wisdom and inner security, with just a peaceful paragraph and an awe-inspiring affirmation. Enjoy a daily dose of reassurance and support with each inspirational offering.

— Rev. Dr. Maxine Kaye

REV. DR. MAXINE KAYE IS THE SPIRITUAL LEADER/SENIOR PASTOR OF THE GREATER PHILADELPHIA CENTER FOR SPIRITUAL LIVING IN PAOLI, PENNSYLVANIA. SHE IS THE AUTHOR OF *ALIVE AND AGELESS: HOW TO FEEL ALIVE AND LIVE FULLY EVERY DAY OF YOUR LIFE.*

PROLOGUE

On January 20, 2017, a palpable wave of fear swept across America, casting a dark shadow over many dear souls in my life, including me. As a spiritual leader in my community, I knew I couldn't idly stand by; I had to do something to assuage the fear. At first, I didn't know what that something was, but after several days of contemplation, it came to me: create a Facebook page called "Fear to Faith" and post daily inspirational thoughts designed to lift the spirits of those who were experiencing this paralyzing dark and sinister fear. My goal was to pull people away from the headlines and into a place of faith so they could feel confident and positive in the midst of unsettling times.

When I began this project, I had no idea that it would turn into a living journal in which I would be intimate and transparent with my readers. What started out as brief, generic inspirational messages turned into my honest and sometimes raw experiences with the vicissitudes of life — and finding a way to use them as a spiritual teaching tool.

When the posts began to change, people started deeply engaging with me and drawing inspiration from my anecdotes. They loved reading about my challenges, triumphs and observations as I walked through a veritable potpourri of experiences. My page became cathartic for me and for others as we discovered the Divine in the midst of this human life.

After some encouragement, those Facebook posts have become this book.

I pray you will find solace in these pages and pick up this book whenever you need your faith restored. The world we live in has never been perfect, and there has always been something troubling regardless of the time in history. Although that "something" has changed over the years, and the fear factor has waxed and waned, its presence has persisted. Fear is part of the human condition regardless of when we live our lives. And if we are going to live in peace, we have to replace fear with faith.

— *Dale Olansky, RScP*

ACKNOWLEDGEMENTS

First and foremost, I must thank my beloved parents who are both on the other side of the veil. They taught me the importance of education and speaking my truth, and this book is a testament to the values they imparted to me. My father, Howard Olansky, was a writer, and he taught me how to hone my skills, much to my chagrin when I was a young girl. My mother, Ilene Olansky, was a paragon of courage and strength, and I thank her for always reminding me that there was nothing I could not do. I am so grateful to them both.

I would like to thank my sister, Ellen Olansky, who is not only my biological sister but my soul sister as well. When I was a lost and confused 17 year-old girl, she taught me what it meant to be spiritual, not religious. I will forever be grateful to her for opening my eyes to my path.

I offer a big thank you to Rev. Dr. Maxine Kaye, who taught me how to be a practitioner of Religious Science. She gently took me over the threshold into sacred service and taught me how to connect with Spirit and pray from my heart.

I am grateful to Rev. Dr. Joe Hooper, who believed in me and gave me countless opportunities to grow myself as a spiritual leader and gain confidence in what is the greatest career I could ever dream of having.

I would like to thank Stephanie Dawn, who lovingly and patiently birthed me into becoming a spiritual entrepreneur.

Thank you to my friend, consultant and content editor, Ginny Weissman, who saw my talent and encouraged me to write this book. What a joy to work with her on this project.

I am indebted to the late Dr. Tom Costa, who cracked my heart open to loving and appreciating myself, when he said, "You are a very valuable, worthwhile person." My life has never been the same since, and I am eternally grateful for the part he played in my spiritual evolution.

Lastly, I am grateful for Center for Spiritual Living Palm Desert for giving me a place to heal my wounds, learn the art of being a practitioner and find my passion.

CONTENTS

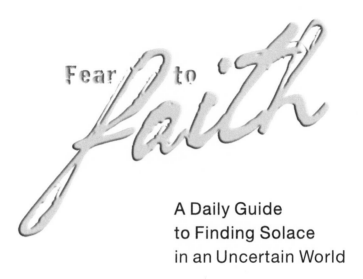

A Daily Guide
to Finding Solace
in an Uncertain World

ABOUT THIS BOOK

Fear to Faith is organized as daily inspirational messages. Each message includes an affirmation, which appears after the message, and is numbered for a full year of inspiration. The messages are undated, giving you flexibility to begin at any point along your own journey from fear to faith. Many pages include room to write your thoughts, your feelings, your own affirmations. Toward a strengthening of your own faith, I offer these messages and wish you safe travels.

Love and Blessings,
Dale Olansky, RScP

We live in a world where we view an excessive number of images on a daily basis, and those images get lodged in our subconscious, influencing our experience of life. Unfortunately, many of those images do not reflect the truth of who we are. When we take a step back and become the observer of those images, we create distance between what we are seeing and who we really are. This allows us to free ourselves from being manipulated by the false messages we receive from the outside world. Something that helps me create this distance is to see the images as if I were looking through a kaleidoscope. Once I put the kaleidoscope down, the images are no longer part of my reality.

I no longer identify with the images that appear in my world that do not resonate with my spirit. I am made of the boundless, invisible energy of God that is beyond anything my eyes can see.

2

Many years ago during a conversation with a trusted friend, I mentioned that I didn't want to worry anymore. Her comment to me was, "Then don't!" I was perplexed by her comment. How could I possibly stop worrying, just like that? The more I thought about it, the more I realized the truth of what she said. We all have the power to choose our thoughts; so yes, I could choose not to worry, just like that. We can apply this truth to fear as well. If you don't want to feel fear anymore, then don't! Choose faith instead.

Today I choose to live in faith as I see the presence of God in everyone and everything. I know I am part of the Divine pattern of the universe, and everything has its purpose. The goodness of God is continually unfolding, so I can rest my mind in faith that all is well.

_____

_____

_____

_____

_____

_____

_____

_____

Fear to *faith*

I have read many articles that say we live in a time where old, dark energies are being healed and dissolved into light. Much of our troubles stem from the unresolved hidden traumas of our past that lurk in the shadows of our consciousness and create discord in our lives. As I watch this play out in the world at large, I think it is the cause of much of the ugliness and inhumanity that we see. As compelling as it is to want to change those who are unconscious of their behavior, the healing actually begins with us individually. God knows I have done a lot of inner work on my past, but I have learned to keep the door open to the possibility that there is more that needs to be revealed and healed. So during this time of healing old, dark energy, I know I have the strength to see whatever needs to be brought into the light so that I can be healed and fully present to this beautiful life Spirit has blessed me to live.

I welcome the revelation of all I need to see that liberates me from old pain that is no longer in my life. My spirit is filled with joy as I welcome a new way of being that is light and free.

_____

_____

_____

_____

4

I used to think that healing was about fixing myself or trying to restore myself to what I was before I needed to heal. Now I see healing as transformation; it is an opportunity to evolve into someone new. Whatever leads to our healing, whether it is a broken heart, a broken body or a broken mind, we are being called to rise up, nourish ourselves and engage in a new vision of wholeness that opens the door for our healing to manifest.

I see healing as an opportunity to transform myself and become a more radiant, vibrant expression of God. I listen to Spirit's guidance as It leads me to that which supports my healing journey.

Fear to *faith*

An idea that brings me great comfort on my spiritual journey is that there are many rooms within the one house we call our mind. I find this idea liberating, especially when I am stuck in a place within myself that is constricting and I need to shift. One of my favorite interior rooms is my "Zen Room." This is the place I go when I don't want to be disturbed by anything discordant or anxiety provoking — a place where I can steep myself in peace. I love my Zen Room because I can just be in my beingness and know that all is well, I am fine, and since the world is governed by Spirit, I can just go with the flow and trust that all is unfolding in its right and perfect way.

My mind has many rooms within it, and I have the ability to choose which rooms I live in. I choose those rooms that bring me great joy and peace.

Fear to *faith*

6

As I was recently thanking God for various things in my life, I was taken aback when I heard myself say, "Thank you, God, for giving me wings." No matter the challenge or lack of faith I have felt during parts of my life, there always came a point when my wings unfolded and I could fly again. I think we are all born with wings, but sometimes life beats us down so much that we forget they are there. Spirit gave us wings to use so we can rise up from any turmoil, confusion or sorrow and soar into the joy of life again.

Spirit gave me the ability to transcend any conditions that keep me mired in lack and limitation. I use my wings to elevate my consciousness so I can float on the current of Spirit's light and love once again.

I find that my faith wavers when I look at what is going on in the world, and I cannot see God. This is just a judgment on my part, because the truth is that God is everywhere present at all times and expresses through all things, beings and situations. As humans, we yearn to see evidence of God as we define it in our external world. I think the evidence is always there; we just have to open our eyes and recognize it. This is where faith comes in. If I think God is not present, I must remember that the evidence I am seeking is emerging from the invisible to the visible. I have to keep the space open for it to come through, and it always does when I have faith.

Today I am able to clearly see the evidence of God in everything and in all situations. I see the Divine in nature and within myself. I stand in faith knowing that evidence of God's presence always comes forward in the most perfect way.

Fear to *faith*

8

There are so many things in our world that are composed of layers — onions, rocks, lasagna and human beings, just to name a few. We are multi-layered organisms in all ways: physically, mentally, spiritually, energetically and emotionally. Having multiple layers to our existence gives us options that allow us to move through our life experiences without having to stay stuck in one place. The deeper we go, the more power is revealed to us. Many people live on the outer layer of consciousness; they only see that which is superficial, external and perceptible to the five senses. I used to be one of those people until I realized there was more to life than what was on the surface. That was the moment I knew it was time for me to take the deep dive into my soul and explore the deeper layers of my beingness to find that which brings so much richness to life.

I take delight in knowing *there are unlimited layers of my beingness that I can explore at any time and discover the unlimited treasures deep within me.*

I have had many conversations with people about their frustrations when things they deeply desire are not manifesting in their lives. Some of the questions I hear are: "Maybe God doesn't want me to have that?" or "Maybe it isn't the right time?" My answer is always that it isn't God standing in the way; it is us. Ernest Holmes said that we have the ability to manifest anything we desire instantly as long as it does not harm anyone. The reason we don't manifest is because we have a deep, subconscious belief standing in the way. The remedy is to begin by setting the intention, praying and/or saying affirmations for the belief(s) to be loosened up and released so that your good can appear in your life. We have the power to free ourselves from limiting beliefs so the Creative Power of the universe can do what It does so well: bring our dreams into concrete form.

Knowing that Spirit always says "yes," I command my subconscious to release any beliefs that stand in the way of the demonstration of my good, allowing my dreams to come forth with ease.

10

As I gazed up at the luminous moon early this morning, I was struck by its light and beauty. I thought about its ever-changing nature as it goes through its different phases and varying shades of colors. As I took a step back, I realized that in reality, the moon never changes at all; it is just a big gray rock orbiting around our earth. Nature is such a great teacher, and here she is, teaching me yet another lesson about the human condition. Just as our position on Earth determines how we see the moon, so our perception colors everything we see in life. We turn the meaningless into meaningful based on what is in our consciousness. Our unlimited capacity to create nothing from something brings great depth to our lives and fills our experiences with substance and value.

As I recognize that I give my life meaning, I see the presence of Spirit's goodness in all that surrounds me.

Fear to faith

The goal of spiritual development is not to get to a place where the vicissitudes of life no longer affect us. In my mind, I think that inner peace, mindfulness and a deeper connection to Spirit are significant goals of spiritual development. In my early years on the spiritual path, I measured my success by how well I could control my emotional reactions to what was happening around me. I thought if I wasn't getting triggered or being moved out of a place of peace, I was doing well.

Today I see things differently. I now define my success by the quality of my resting energy. If my baseline energy is peaceful, harmonious and loving, then my spiritual work is working. I know life happens, and things come up that affect me, and I'm ok with that. I don't mind feeling sad, angry, frustrated, etc., because I know how to return to my peaceful resting energy after I have fully processed an experience. This allows me to accept my humanity and be who I am because I know I always come home to peace.

My resting energy is calm and peaceful. *I am able to easily return to it after any experience.*

12

When I was a child, I came to the conclusion that my parents didn't really love each other because their behavior did not match my definition of love. They did not show affection toward each other, they argued a lot, they were angry. Two days ago, I realized I was wrong. My assumption was not correct; they did love each other, they just did not show it outwardly. My childhood assessment caused me to weave a tapestry of belief around love and marriage, and now that belief is unraveling because I pulled the thread of untruth that held it all together. This realization caused me to think about how many other beliefs I may have that are being held together by a thread of untruth. So much to think about.

I open myself up to seeing any threads of untruth that are holding beliefs in place that do not serve me. As the tapestries of those beliefs unravel, the light of truth is revealed, and I am submerged in the joy of enlightenment.

_____

_____

_____

_____

_____

Fear to *faith*

I was catching up with a friend when she suddenly turned the conversation toward me personally, and I was thrust into a place of frenetic mental query. After she said the words, "Now, I don't want you to get hurt by what I am about to say," time stood still. Before she could even get to the next part of her statement, my mind immediately went into hyper-drive as I tried to prepare myself for what she was going to say. A million questions darted through my mind: What could she say that would hurt me? Can I handle feeling bad about myself? Is my self-concept going to be turned upside down?

As I realized there was nothing I could do but brace myself for what I was about to hear, I reminded myself that it is up to me if I allow her words to hurt me or not. As it turned out, her comment was benign, but my mind took me on quite a ride.

As the master of my consciousness, I have the power to accept or reject any opinions that others may have of me. I am Spirit in form, and knowing that creates an impenetrable barrier that protects me from being hurt by anyone's words.

14

This morning I felt really boxed in within my mind, and I couldn't figure out how to go beyond what I was experiencing. I asked myself: Where is my Source? I knew I needed to look to a higher form of energy to get free from what I was experiencing. As soon as I asked the question, my consciousness shifted, and I was able to look beyond my mind for liberation. By activating my awareness of the presence of Spirit, I felt new life surging from deep within me, as the box I was in dissolved. The simple act of recognizing our Higher Power is a huge catalyst that moves us from fear to faith, from chaos to order, from stagnation to movement, from bondage to freedom.

The road to inner freedom begins when I recognize my divine partnership with Spirit. I go to the one Source of life with an open and receptive heart, and It gives of Itself abundantly providing me with the ways and means to rejuvenate myself.

_____

_____

_____

_____

_____

_____

Fear to *faith*

Yesterday I had lunch with a dear friend, and we had the most amazing demonstration of abundance from beginning to end. Not only were we given extra goodies during our meal, but as we were leaving the restaurant, the owner gave us a special gift. As I marveled at this wonderful outpouring of goodness, I reminded myself that when you freely give of yourself to others, it comes back to you when you least expect it. I have done a lot of work on myself to receive as graciously as I give so that I can continually be in the flow of Spirit's goodness. God created us to live in harmony with the Law of Reciprocity so that we are never wanting for anything. When we balance our ability to fully enjoy both giving and receiving, we always have plenty of everything.

I experience deep joy when I give and receive, and my world is filled with abundance. As I open myself up to being the inflow and outflow of Spirit's gifts in all Its forms, I am amazed at the bounty of goodness that shows up in my life, and I share my good with others.

16

One of my favorite childhood memories was when my mom tucked me in bed at night. I always felt safe and secure as I drifted into sleep. I find myself recalling this memory today because our world is a little scary right now. Whatever I can do to connect with a feeling of safety and security puts me on the right track to restoring my inner peace. Remembering how I felt when mom tucked me in at night brings me to the awareness that I can feel safe no matter what is going on around me.

My mind is filled with peace as I turn my attention to the all-encompassing Spirit that reminds me that my soul is always safe and secure no matter what is going on in this world.

_____

_____

_____

_____

_____

_____

_____

_____

_____

_____

Fear to *faith*

It is comforting to be around people who "get" us — our loved ones who know us inside and out and love and support us unconditionally. Those of us who do not follow the average way of being in this world are prone to feelings of alienation, which may cause us to question ourselves. As wonderful as it is to have people in our lives who counter those feelings by supporting us in our individuality, it is incumbent upon us to accept ourselves and stand strong in who we are without hesitation in the face of feeling different from the masses. We must appreciate that which makes us unique rather than doubt ourselves. In order to live in peace, we have to "get" who we are and love ourselves unconditionally.

I understand myself and appreciate the unique expression of Spirit that I am. I live my life in a constant state of wholeness and peace, and I shine my light wherever I am.

18

During a class I attended, one of the students presented us with a picture of the spectrum of all life that included the invisible and the visible, and it showed that our eyes can only see a sliver of all that exists. This strengthened my faith because what my eyes see right now, specifically with our government, disturbs me. Knowing that there is something positive unfolding that my eyes cannot see brings me great peace, for I know that God is the Invisible Presence that brings everything back into perfect balance.

Today I trust that Spirit is restoring peace, order and balance to our world. Even though I cannot see this with my eyes, my heart knows this is true.

Fear to *faith*

As much as I love words and the language they create, there is another language I am even more fond of that is beyond words, symbols and sounds: the language of the soul. This language has no tangible form for it is a language of feeling and intuition. When I take time out of my day to just sit in silence and turn away from the happenings of this world, I am able to hear this language as the sweet whisper of Spirit singing Its song of love into my heart. Time stands still, and the weight of the world leaves my mind. The language of the soul pierces through the veil of the temporal world, where our attention is fixed, revealing the divine nature of life. Our vision is cleansed, and our minds are relaxed as we realize that all is well for everything is under the care and guidance of Infinite Intelligence.

As I turn within to listen to the language of my soul, I feel the presence of God, and peace and harmony are restored within me.

20

I believe it is our nature to live in harmony. Something that can pull us out of a harmonious state of being is entanglement. When our thoughts and emotions get attached to and tangled up in situations and circumstances that are unhealthy and out of our control, we experience constriction and stress. Awareness is the best remedy for getting ourselves untangled. When we can see our entanglement, we can untangle ourselves and return to a state of harmony.

Today I consciously untangle myself *from any thought, emotion, person or situation that constricts the flow of my life force. My harmony is now restored, and I can enjoy this day in freedom.*

Fear to *faith*

Every human being is like a planet in the cosmos; each one has its own atmosphere, orbit and life forms. Given the number and variety of all the "people planets" living on our one planet, it is amazing that we have the harmony we do. Given my propensity for turning inward, I find that sometimes I need to look outside my own planet and take notice of the other planets in the same galaxy. To observe the unique qualities of others as though they are planets orbiting the great sun of Spirit allows me to see people with a broader perspective and without judgment.

We are all unique planets in the universe of humanity, *perfectly balanced in our oneness as we orbit the light of Spirit together.*

Fear to *faith*

22

I know a lot of people right now who have hit their stress threshold because life has become too much, and they see no end to situations that are causing them discord. In his book *The Untethered Soul,* Michael Singer explains that the solution to the pressures of life is not in fixing that which is outside of us but in changing our reactions to those circumstances. That brings me great relief, because it puts the power to change my experience in my hands rather than having to wait to feel better until the situation outside of me changes. We all have the power to disengage from stress and draw on the peace of Spirit to give us the relief we are seeking. The choice is ours.

I no longer allow external situations that are beyond my control to rob me of my peace. I anchor my consciousness in the ever-present serenity that lies deep within my soul, and I am able to walk through my life with a peaceful heart.

_____

_____

_____

_____

_____

_____

_____

Fear to *faith*

23

Yesterday I felt disappointed in myself because I thought I could have done a better job on some things I have been working on. My mind started to take me down the rabbit hole where I beat myself up for not being perfect. As the self-talk started with statements such as, "You should have known better," I stopped myself and said, "Enough!", I realized that getting down on myself serves no purpose, and I don't want to waste any more of my precious life tearing myself apart.

It became clear to me that I was just repeating an old pattern I learned when I was a child: When mistakes are made, punishment follows. I decided to create a new pattern when I make mistakes or fall short of my personal expectations: Just figure out how I can do better next time.

I no longer indulge in self-punishing thoughts, for that is no way to treat an expression of Spirit. I use my mind constructively and affirmatively whenever I desire self-improvement, knowing I will manifest wonderful results by keeping my consciousness in the flow of harmony and love.

24

This week I hit the proverbial wall because I overloaded myself with too many responsibilities. I am humbled by this experience because I had to admit to myself that I can't say "yes" to everything anymore. I have limits. I could blame this on aging, but I don't think that is what lies underneath this shift. I think I have come to a point in my life where I can no longer override the need for inner balance. In the past, when that balance was tipped, I was able to ignore it; now I can't.

I have come to the realization that I require substantial unstructured time for balance. I know this is a good thing, and I am grateful I have created a flexible life with God's guidance.

As I connect with the Source of my being, I am empowered to live a balanced life that is peaceful and harmonious.

I used to think I had to go back into my personal history to figure out why I was feeling a certain way so I could change how I felt. Today I am questioning that theory. This morning I wasn't comfortable in the energy I was feeling, but instead of going into self-analysis, I just chose to detach from that energy and substitute it with the energy I wanted to experience. After a few times of going back and forth between the two states of being, my energy stayed exactly where I wanted it to be. I didn't have to analyze my thoughts or get introspective. I just chose a different feeling state, and that became my reality.

I am able to feel exactly how I want to feel simply by using the power of choice. Spirit has given me the ability to create my inner atmosphere, and outer circumstances cannot take that freedom away from me.

Fear to *faith*

26

Sometimes we find it challenging to see the beauty and vibrancy that rests deep within our own souls. If we keep our focus on whatever gloom and doom may be outside of us, then we are blind to the endless reservoir of goodness that dwells in our interior world. Within all of us lies a beautiful inner garden in which we can find peace and solace — no matter what is going on in the world outside of us. It is a place that is always in bloom, because it is where the eternal nature of our beingness resides. Whenever I need to restore my faith and connection with Spirit, I go to this place, and I am fed just what my soul needs to be renewed.

Today I look upon my soul as an inner garden in which I plant the seeds of love, truth, beauty and wisdom. I nurture my inner garden with my faith. This garden is a place I can go to whenever I need rejuvenation and peace. No matter what is going on in the outside world, I know the world within me is flourishing.

Fear to *faith*

The concept of the "dark night of the soul" invokes a sense of heaviness around it, and for good reason. During those times in life when we get stuck feeling lost, abandoned and hopeless, we must expend great effort to get out of that consciousness. Regardless of the experience that brings on the dark night, in my mind, there is only one universal cause: separation from our Higher Power. When we have an experience that pushes us to doubt the presence of Spirit, we go dark. This inner drama is created by the mind because our expectation of how God is supposed to show up in our lives has not been met.

When that dark night arises, the healing lies in changing our understanding of Spirit and using the Law of Mind. Instead of seeing adversity as the absence of God, we must remember that adversity cannot damage our spirit, and God is with us through thick and thin. Then we must use the creative process through prayer or just by knowing and having faith. Then we can activate the energy of the Universe to bring solutions and goodness into our experience.

I use my consciousness to keep the light of Spirit alive in my life regardless of anything I am experiencing. As I realize that nothing is fixed and the possibility for change is always present, I lean into God to transform anything that is dark into light.

Fear to *faith*

28

Today is a really good day to be drenched in love. I am so grateful that many years ago I learned that I don't need to have something outside of myself to elicit the feeling of love. Within all of us is an endless supply of unconditional love that we can tap into and draw on at any time. It comes from Spirit, and it is the essence of our being. Love is the greatest healing balm in the Universe, and when we vibrate in the frequency of love, that vibration travels all over the world and impacts all life.

I bathe myself in the loving energy of Spirit, and it fills me up with joy and goes out into the world and softens all hearts.

Fear to *faith*

Today is one of those days when I feel like I am pushing a big heavy rock that seems impossible to move. I know I can't move the things that are going on outside of me that appear stuck, so I have to move the only thing I have control of — my thoughts. As simple as that sounds, it actually requires effort because I have to plant the seed of thought I would like to experience, and then I must tend to it by nurturing it with faith and weeding out the thoughts that do not support my intention. This can be a sensitive time because if we do not see what we want to see in the time-frame we expect to see it, we can lose faith. However, we have the whole universe behind us when we set our intention. We cannot fail.

I turn over all my burdens to the universe for transformation. I know that Spirit can move mountains, so I leave the heavy lifting for It to do. With joyous expectation, I now receive the most amazing demonstrations of Spirit's goodness, and my mind returns to peace.

_____

_____

_____

_____

_____

Fear to *faith*

30

Today I caught myself falling into us/them thinking, and when I realized how awful I was feeling, I said to myself, "Enough!" I knew I needed to change my perception and see oneness instead of division and open up my heart to see the common bonds we share. There is a lot of messaging happening in our world right now that encourages separation and fear of each other, and it is our responsibility to reject that message. It is time for us all to dig deep and understand anyone we may be judging with contempt. Understanding doesn't mean we condone questionable behavior; it means we reach into our hearts and find compassion, for we don't know what they have endured in their lifetimes.

I open my heart to have compassion for all beings, knowing we are all one. I see Spirit moving through all life and restoring our collective wholeness.

Fear to *faith*

One of the things I love about spiritual work is that the results just sneak up on you when you least expect them. At one point during my day yesterday, I realized something was missing, and that something was inner chatter and self-judgment. I realized I had let go of some thought or belief that hindered my self-esteem and weakened my connection to Spirit. I wish I could remember what it was, but I can't. The important thing is that it is gone. This is a reminder to me as to why I continue doing my daily spiritual practices and my inner work. Even though I get impatient because my little mind wants all my thoughts and beliefs cleaned up immediately, I know the day always arrives when the results of my work show up in a big way, and a deeper sense of inner freedom becomes my reality.

My spiritual expansion is forever unfolding, and I honor the time it takes for me to let go of that which no longer serves me.

_____

_____

_____

_____

_____

_____

Fear to *faith*

32 Many of us are pulled in so many directions during the day that we can easily get off balance and lose our grounding. Stress and strain over work, getting our tasks accomplished and dealing with unexpected issues can cause us to fragment and forget about that which is always holding us together: Spirit. When the whirlwind of life pulls me off my center, I know it is time for me to step back, be still and connect with my heart. This allows me to bring all of my energy back to the center of my being so I can return to a place of wholeness.

Living in a state of equilibrium allows me to move through my day with complete peace and grace. I nourish all parts of myself that need to be fed, and my soul is filled with delight.

_____

_____

_____

_____

_____

_____

_____

_____

_____

The application of quantum physics on consciousness is massively appealing for it gives us the science that allows us to break free from the limitations of time and space so we can create a life we once thought impossible. The old paradigm of thought keeps us inextricably bound to the past and the reality we created for ourselves based on what we learned about how life works. The only thing that keeps that in place is our minds. How liberating to know that we can abruptly break the old belief systems by knowing we live in a universe of vast possibilities. This opens the door for a new reality to emerge that brings us great joy and freedom.

Knowing that I am unbound by any reality I have ever created for myself, I call upon the quantum energy of Spirit to dissolve any beliefs that limit me, and I joyously enter into a new reality of life.

34

Setting intentions is crucial to creating the life we want to experience; but something that is not often spoken about is examining the intention behind the intention. For example, I know someone who has been yearning to be a professional public speaker for years, and even though she set her intention and does a lot of visualization, she has yet to book a paid speaking gig. The issue is the intention behind her intention. Her primary motivation for becoming a public speaker is to be the center of attention and receive massive praise, because at the depth of her being, she does not love and accept herself. Her intention is coming from a place of lack, which is out of alignment with God. When the intention behind our intentions is rooted in spiritual truth, our intentions manifest quickly and effortlessly.

I am mindful of the intention behind my intentions, and I am able to see which are based on truth and which are not. I only choose intentions that are rooted in Spirit, and they demonstrate with grace and ease.

_____

_____

_____

_____

I was recently talking with someone who has an extraordinarily challenging situation with his son's behavior. During our conversation, he told me that a professional said his son could be "fixed." I know hearing that was a relief to him, but I also knew in my heart that people don't get fixed; they grow and transform, and that can be messy and take time. If we ever find ourselves wanting a person to be fixed, we must accept that it is our consciousness that needs to be fixed.

Everyone is on his or her own path, and even though we may have good solutions that can help a person heal, it is not our job to fix anyone. The best thing we can do is love and support people on their journeys and trust that all is unfolding in the right and perfect way and time through Divine Intelligence.

I recognize that no one is broken and in need of being fixed, for we are all continually evolving beings on this wonderful journey called life. God is the great Presence that guides us through all the twists and turns of life, providing us with the ways and means to transform ourselves.

36

I absolutely love those moments when someone says something to me that would have torn me apart in the past, but that doesn't now.

I just want to jump up and down with joy because the trigger is gone. I have come to realize that the more my self-confidence and self-love increase, the less I am affected by the opinions of others.

When we believe in ourselves and trust ourselves, no one can harm us with their words or judgments. Strong self-love creates a barrier that prevents us from absorbing the opinions and judgments of others. The greatest healing we can do for ourselves is to create a foundation of impenetrable unconditional love and support for ourselves. This is power.

I love and appreciate myself knowing that Spirit endowed me with all Its qualities to express in my own unique way. As I stand in my power, no one and nothing can change how I feel about myself.

_____

_____

_____

_____

_____

_____

The morning glory's flowers unfurl as the sun rises so they can soak up its life-giving energy the entire day, giving the plant the nutrients it needs to thrive. As evening comes, the flowers wilt and die as they have served their purpose. As the next day begins, new flowers appear and repeat this never-ending cycle. I love the metaphor of the morning glory: We are all plants with unlimited possibilities of beauty stored within ourselves, but if we do not allow those possibilities to unfurl and take in the light of Spirit, we cannot thrive. Allowing our unique expression of who we are to blossom and see the light of day gives us the opportunity to be self-expressed, which is what this life is all about. And just like the morning glory, there is no end to the expression of beauty that lies deep within us.

I recognize the never-ending creative nature of my soul as I let my inner beauty blossom and express itself in the world.

_____

_____

_____

_____

_____

_____

38

Whenever we have a dramatic life change, whether desired or not, our inner landscape shifts. Old patterns of thought, perceptions and habits must give way as the new rises up before us.

I realized today that with my recent life change, I entered into a labyrinth that I must walk through in order to process that which changed. The labyrinth can be challenging, for the passage through it is not a clear straight line. Rather it is a complicated maze-like path without road signs. The path requires deep thought and concentration.

For us to successfully navigate our inner labyrinths, we must have awareness, faith, grace and strength so we can find our way out and into the new expanded life that joyfully awaits us.

I honor my journey through change knowing that Spirit has given me the ability to successfully walk through any inner labyrinth that is before me.

When anything or anyone leaves our lives, an empty space opens up. How we deal with that space determines our future. I know many people right now who are dealing with the empty space, including myself. I have come to see the space as bittersweet. It is a place where I feel sad for that which is no longer, but it is also a place that is replete with creative possibility.

When I feel the empty space, the first thing I do is remind myself that I am not alone. Knowing that Spirit is forever present relaxes me to be open to the newness that is born in this space. Having trust in the invisible presence of Spirit when the concrete has disappeared takes great courage and faith. But when we open up to It, the empty space disappears.

Knowing that Spirit is the All-In-All, I feel Its presence whenever I experience change in my life. Nature abhors a vacuum, so I know that God eternally fills all empty spaces with goodness.

40

In the midst of anything we walk through, there is always something to be grateful for. Finding the gratitude in life's challenges allows us to move through the challenge more quickly, opens the space for creative solutions to emerge and restores our well-being. If we can discover just one thing to be grateful for in a difficult experience, we are taking the first step in transforming that experience. And besides, being grateful feels so good.

Just stating five things you are grateful for not only turns your mood around, but doing so will turn around your entire life.

Today I live in gratitude for all the good that is present in my life. Living in gratitude brings more good into my life to be grateful for. I am grateful I am here to see another day. I am grateful for Spirit's love, support and guidance. I am grateful I know that peace and love are stronger than anything else in this world.

_____

_____

_____

_____

_____

In ancient Chinese culture, the legend of the koi fish is an amazing story of transformation. One day, a school of koi set off on an upstream journey to reach enlightenment, only to be met by countless obstacles. However, determined to achieve their goal, they reached their destination, the top of a waterfall, where the gods rewarded them for their perseverance by turning them into dragons.

Sometimes when I am walking through challenge and adversity, I forget that I am on a journey of personal transformation and in the process of turning into someone new. With each obstacle comes the release of old ways of thinking and worn-out attachments that free me to become a whole new person.

Spirit reminds me *that nestled within my soul is a greater expression of life for me, born through adversity.*

42

The story of "Ali Baba and the Forty Thieves" has some fascinating metaphysical components to it, but the part that stands out for me today is the cave that houses an abundant treasure that can only be opened when you say, "Open sesame." When I looked up the etymology of "sesame" and saw that it means "open thyself," the metaphysician in me was filled with delight. When we look for the treasures of our soul, only we alone can open the door to the goodness that lies within us. No one else knows our personal password that grants us access. Many of us on the spiritual path look to others to open up the inner cave that reveals our spiritual treasures buried deep within us, but we have to use our personal soul language to access it.

I easily access my spiritual treasures when I stand in the authentic divine nature of my soul.

Fear to *faith*

I have always enjoyed the wind, primarily because I see it as a representation of Spirit in action, an invisible force making itself known without form. Most people I know do not like the wind because of its destructive nature. Oftentimes, wind creates unexpected changes, just as life naturally does. Our response to the winds of change is everything. Like the saying goes, we can either build a wall to keep it out in the hopes that we will not be affected by it, or we can harness its power and put it to good use. Let's face it: Life gets windy at times, but those winds are Spirit in action, and when we use that energy in positive and productive ways instead of resisting, great things happen.

I see the winds of change as necessary for greater good to come forth in my ever-evolving life.

44

As I was enjoying a wonderful musical yesterday, my mind was drawn to the part of the set with a door that led into the family's home. The grandmother coming through the door transported me back to a precious time in my life and a precious door — the door to my grandmother's apartment. When I was a child, I remember the joy that filled my soul when we went to visit her. It started as soon as we got out of the car and I saw her door. Knowing what was just on the other side of that door — unconditional love and endless nurturing — was everything to me.

That door disappeared from my life many decades ago, but I have a new door that I open that brings the same qualities into my life, and that is the door to Spirit. Behind that door lives love, peace, joy, prosperity, wholeness and wisdom, and I can go there whenever I need to be filled up and reminded about the truth of who I am.

The door to Spirit is always open *to me as It provides me with a place to go to refresh my soul and bring balance back into my life.*

Fear to *faith*

Much of the work I do involves lifting people out of pain and despair so their faith can be restored and they can jump back into the flow of life with joy. I must confess that there are moments when I just want to wave my magic wand and make everyone's pain go away. I'm sure many of you have felt that way in your lives with your friends and loved ones. Whenever I feel this way, I have to remember that behind all suffering is the opportunity for a break-through, and my job isn't to make anything go away, but rather to show people how to find the light within that is beckoning them to heal.

I freely give my love and support to all who suffer, knowing that the Spirit within provides healing simply by my recognizing Its presence and Its ability to do so.

_____

_____

_____

_____

_____

_____

_____

_____

46

I don't hide from the reality that there are a lot of harsh things happening in the world. However, I know that I am responsible for my reactions to what I see. Today I started to react with anger to something I saw, and I realized I am tired of feeling this way. I made the decision to react differently by meeting the adversity with a soft heart. I opened up to love, trusting that Spirit is working everything out. Although this may not be easy, it brings great peace.

Today I meet all adversity with a soft heart, and fear and discord melt away. I have complete faith that the divine action of Spirit brings harmony into our world.

Fear to *faith*

There are times in life when a new experience presents itself that seems daunting, and we may think we don't have the ability to walk through it because it is just too much to handle. This applies to a wide variety of situations: changing careers, getting over loss or falling in love, just to name a few. When I find myself bumping against the thought, "I can't do this," I say this mantra: "I am well-equipped to handle this situation. Spirit gave me the tools and ability to do this and to do it well." When I remind myself of this truth, my energy shifts, and I realize I truly can move through the situation with ease because I have everything I need within me to do anything that is before me.

Spirit gave me all the strength and wisdom I need to comfortably move through all life experiences.

Fear to faith

48

For months, I procrastinated about trimming the palm tree in my back yard. The poor tree was weighted down with dead palm fronds, and its energy was being drained by something that had no life and needed to be removed. Yesterday I finally got motivated and trimmed at least 25 dead palm fronds off the tree. It is wonderful to see the tree brimming with life now that all of its energy is available to feed that which is vibrant and alive.

I couldn't help but see this is as a life lesson. How often do we allow that which is no longer life-affirming to stay attached to us, whether it is an old thought pattern, a relationship or our identity? We get weighted down and depleted because our energy is going into something that is no longer affirming. It is time for us to trim our personal dead palm fronds so our energy can be directed toward that which is life-sustaining, allowing us to grow and thrive.

I am ready to release anything I have been holding onto that does not support my spirit, and my entire being is restored and revitalized.

_____

_____

_____

Fear to *faith*

As we do our inner work and restore our power and wholeness, that which is toxic in our lives becomes clear. As wonderful as this clarity is, we may have to make some difficult decisions about eliminating that which is harmful to us, especially if it is in the form of a relationship with a family member, a spouse or a friend. It can be overwhelming to even consider the next step to take. Whenever I come to this crossroad in my life, the first thing I do is allow myself to just rest in what is before me and give myself permission to take my time in figuring out what I am going to do. I then imagine my life without the person in it and how that would feel, and I just let myself bathe in that feeling. The last thing I do is release the situation to Spirt knowing It is providing me with the perfect solution.

I honor myself by letting go of unhealthy relationships knowing that God shows me the best path to take to peacefully release them. This opens the door for new loving people to come into my life.

_____

_____

_____

_____

_____

50

Instead of just letting life happen to us and reacting to it all, let's take charge and declare the good we would like to experience in our lives.

Spirit gave us free will to choose our path, so let's have some fun and call forth that which we would like to experience. I am knowing for all of you that those choices include perfect health and wellness, unlimited energy, unobstructed creativity, joy, prosperity and loving harmonious relationships.

Today I look within my heart and set my intentions for this day, knowing Spirit acts on them and brings them forth in the perfect way. I am grateful God has blessed me so abundantly.

Fear to *faith*

We humans play a lot of mind games with ourselves when it comes to our divine power. A friend of mind recently told me that when she touches a certain spiritual book in her library, she feels the power of the book, which in turn makes her feel spiritually connected. I must confess that sometimes I fall into the belief that certain things serve as a catalyst to make me feel more spiritually connected. There really is no harm in this belief. Sometimes when we feel disconnected from Spirit it helps to have something concrete to psychologically reconnect us. However, the truth is that we can never be separated from God, and we don't need anything to invoke Its presence because we are Its presence in human form. These things we use to connect us to Spirit are powerless in and of themselves; the spiritual power we seek is already in us because we are it. We don't need books or crystals or anything to restore that power; we just need to remember that we are the Power, and It can never be taken away from us.

Recognizing the divine nature of my beingness is all I need to feel the power of my spirit.

_____

_____

_____

Fear to *faith*

52

Many people do not know that when I left my childhood home at age 19 and ventured out into the world of adulthood, I had no self-esteem and my inner light was dim. I was lost inside, did not know who I was, and I had no idea what I wanted to do with my life. My relationship with Spirit was weak, so I felt completely alone. In the midst of all that inner chaos, I knew I needed to just go out into the world and experience life beyond all that I had ever known. I knew that life would be my teacher, and I would find what I was looking for by meeting new people and being exposed to things I had never seen before. In time, I was able to create an inner environment drenched in love of self and others, and this allowed me to feel worthy and deserving of God's presence in my life. I came to realize that I did not want to walk my path without God, so I opened up to doing whatever I needed to do to heal the gap between me and Spirit.

As I see all the people who are silently suffering in our world and making harmful decisions to end that suffering, it reminds me of my journey through darkness. There is clearly a deep spiritual crisis rampant in our world right now, and as we struggle to figure out how to solve this problem, the solution is actually simple: love. However, the journey to love is not so simple. The good news is that we can help by being the presence of love for all beings. Sometimes a loving gesture can change a person's world forever.

Today and every day I show up as love and share my heart with all who cross my path. Love truly is the greatest healer, and I pray that all who suffer can open themselves up to the love that is deep within them.

Fear to *faith*

No one really uses the word "firmament" much in today's world. It is a word found in the Bible, and it refers to the celestial heavens that exist above us, the place where Spirit lives. When I looked up the origins of the word, I was fascinated to learn that it means "strengthen, support." To view the heavens—which are commonly depicted as a formless, ethereal realm—as a place that is grounding and supportive intrigued me. If we interpret the heavens as our higher consciousness — the place within ourselves where we can access a greater wisdom beyond this world and see it as a place of support and strength — that reinforces the idea that our true stability lies in the unseen, invisible aspect of our beingness, not in the earthly realm.

I know my true strength lies within the higher consciousness of my being where I can access the Mind of God for my inner stability and security.

Fear to *faith*

54

Every day seems to bring something new for us to process. Rather than resist what is, it behooves us to be like a willow tree in the wind and bend. As the quote by an unknown author says, "Allow yourself to bend like a willow in the wind so that you will not break." This is a time to connect with the root of who we are and let Spirit support us through these strange times. There is impenetrable strength and resilience within each one us, and we are being given the opportunity to call it forth to ground us through this experience.

My spirit is flexible, as I calmly experience the changing world in which I live. I recognize the indestructible force of Spirit that dwells within me, knowing It gives me the fortitude and strength to thrive no matter what is going on around me.

_____

_____

_____

_____

_____

_____

_____

_____

Fear to *faith*

Today the message from the universe is: Lighten up! Doesn't it feel good to contemplate that thought? There is more to life than being serious. We need to have fun, so take some time today to indulge in something playful and bring a little light into your soul.

I give myself permission to be playful today and see the amusement of life. Knowing that everything is governed by Spirit, I don't need to control anything today. I release all burdens I may carry, and relax into the wonder of this life.

Fear to *faith*

56

We are all born with an inner compass that is ours to use to help guide us through life. This compass is calibrated with our heart and God, so it gives us perfect directions for living a life that is meaningful and fulfilling. However, we may have forgotten this truth and allowed someone or something outside of ourselves to be our compass. When this happens, we eventually get lost.

Today I restore my connection to my inner compass, and I can clearly see the direction my life is to proceed for my greatest good to unfold. Decisions come easily for I trust my inner compass. Peace and freedom are now mine as I live my life in tune with my divine nature.

Fear to *faith*

A powerful saying in New Thought is, "The Universe is for me, not against me." When I was first introduced to this idea, I struggled with it. Having been raised Jewish, I thought just the opposite. I was taught that I was part of a religion that was reviled by many people, and I was never safe. I didn't like living with this mindset so, when I came into New Thought, I gave this new idea a chance even though it was contrary to my mental programming. After much work, I finally embodied this idea, and I no longer live in fear. Even though I recognize there is hate and anger in our world, I don't take it on or allow it to cripple me.

As I embrace the idea that the universe is for me, not against me, I let go of all fear and experience deep peace. Spirit is the greatest power there is, and as I lean into It, I am able to relax into my life.

Fear to *faith*

58

I think many of us have experienced moments in our lives when we questioned our ability to handle a challenging situation. What I know to be true is that God has given all of us a strong and resilient spirit to be able to walk through any challenge and come out unscathed on the other side.

Deep within me lies an unshakeable Presence *that gives me all the strength and ability to move through any experience with ease. This place is where Spirit lives, and It supports me throughout my life. I relax into this Presence, and It gives me all I need to meet any challenge I may be facing.*

Fear to *faith*

When insanity looms large before your very eyes, what do you do? It is clearly a moment to choose faith over fear. Appearances are fleeting, and when we stand in faith and trust the power of Infinite Intelligence to bring order in the midst of chaos, we can walk through any experience with a peaceful heart.

Today I deepen my faith and trust that Spirit is bringing balance to the world in which I live. I don't allow anyone or anything to rob me of my power, as I remain solid in my faith. I trust that all is unfolding through the grace of God, and I relax in this truth.

60

This morning I woke up feeling all tangled up in my mind. As much as I enjoy having a brain, there are moments when there is way too much activity going on there, and my circuits get tangled. When this happens, I know it is a call for me to move my attention from my mind to my heart. The energy of the heart smooths everything out and restores us to peace.

Today I give my mind a break by moving my awareness to the center of my being — my heart. The heart is where God lives within me, and I now commune with this Divine Presence that stills my soul and brings me peace. I gladly let go of all stress so I can receive the spiritual nourishment that brings my spirit back to life.

Fear to *faith*

Each one of us has an inner narrator constantly running in the background of our mind, providing us with narration in the form of commentary and judgment about ourselves and our world. What is your inner narrator telling you about yourself and your life? Is it telling you things that are scaring you or giving you faith? Is it time to give it a new script to read?

Today I monitor my inner narrator to make sure it only speaks words of faith and love to me. I have the power to change its script if need be. I choose the narration of my mind to be positive and life affirming.

62

Traveling to places we have never been enriches our lives by exposing us to new scenery and people. However, there is another form of travel that is less popular, and that is inner travel. There is so much uncharted land that lies within us to explore, and it doesn't cost anything to go there. When we take this journey, we are able to see the untapped lush territory that lies within us.

Today I explore the inner terrain of my consciousness, and I am delighted to see the wonderful places within myself I did not know existed. With Spirit as my travel guide, I know I will be taken to only the finest destinations.

_____

_____

_____

_____

_____

_____

_____

_____

_____

_____

_____

_____

Our world is seriously lacking leaders
with integrity and grace, and only a precious
few rise to the status of hero. The solution?
We need to become our own heroes. Every one of us
is a hero. Every life is a heroic journey, and the time has
come for us to recognize this and honor the hero within.

I see my life as a hero's journey, and I appreciate all I have
experienced for it has made me the person I am today. I see
myself as strong, brave and persevering, knowing I have
triumphed over much adversity. I am my own hero.

Fear to *faith*

64

We all have the unlimited capacity to dream, but sometimes we dismiss our dreams as too big or impossible. When that happens, we let them die inside of us. Dreams are put on our hearts for a reason. They are the Divine Urge within us seeking expression through us. If you have dreams that seem complicated and out of reach, don't give up. Let Spirit figure out the how, and listen for the divine guidance that brings forth your dreams into the world.

Today I allow myself to listen to the dreams nestled within me, and as I listen to Spirit's guidance, the perfect path unfolds for my dreams to be realized.

Fear to *faith*

Sometimes I grow weary of waiting for things to shift in my life. I just want everything to change — NOW! Do you ever feel like that? The call to be patient is not always easy to heed, but it is a must. There is a greater intelligence governing our individual lives and all life, and there is a lot of orchestrating taking place behind the scenes so that everything unfolds for the greatest good. We certainly don't want the universe to rush things just because we are feeling impatient.

I have faith that the Mind of God is governing *the activity of my life, so I relax in the knowing that everything is unfolding through divine order. I am grateful I can see God's handiwork in all that is happening in my life.*

_____

_____

_____

_____

_____

_____

_____

_____

_____

Fear to *faith*

66

I truly believe that all fear and discord are caused by a disconnection with Spirit. When we feel in tune with that which is greater than ourselves and trust that there is a Divine Intelligence that governs our lives and the universe, we are at peace. However, when we don't like what we see in our lives or what is happening in the world, our faith may weaken. When I experience this, I remind myself that life is like a movie, and this is just one scene. Knowing that God is the Great Director, I realize this is just part of a bigger story with a happy ending.

Today I connect with God in a deeper way, as I redefine what It is to me, and see how It shows up in my daily life. I no longer base my faith on the external reality in which I live, but rather I base my faith on the love I feel in my heart. I know that when I am anchored in God, I create a better life for myself and the world.

_____

_____

_____

_____

_____

_____

Fear to *faith*

Do you ever stop to acknowledge the wonderful person you are? It is easy for most of us to shower praise on others but not on ourselves. Some of us shrink at the thought of commending ourselves, maybe because we think that would be arrogant, or maybe we were taught that it is wrong to give ourselves kudos. The time has come for us to change our attitude toward ourselves and celebrate the magnificent beings we are.

Today I honor myself and all I have achieved throughout my lifetime. I appreciate the unique expression of God that I am. I am proud to be me. I am grateful for my life, and I take nothing for granted. Life is a gift, and I celebrate the divine being that I am.

68

We have more control over our thinking than we know. It is a common misconception that we are stuck with our mental patterns. The truth is that our minds are pliable, and we can change how we think. The first step is slowing down our thoughts so we can see what we are thinking. Once we do that, we can make any changes we like to our consciousness.

Today I choose to be the master of my mind by becoming the observer of what I am thinking. I no longer indulge in thoughts of fear and anxiety. Instead I choose to immerse myself in faith and love. My life is peaceful when I carefully choose my thoughts.

I find great comfort when I remember these words: This, too, shall pass. Whenever I think that things are going in a scary direction, I remind myself that nothing is fixed. Everything is fluid and changeable, and my consciousness influences the direction of how everything unfolds, not only in my personal life but in global life as well. This is why it is vitally important for all of us to keep ourselves centered in faith and optimism. Then we can hold the collective knowing that the goodness of Spirit is dissolving all that does not vibrate at Its level.

I am calm and peaceful as I remember that everything in life is changeable, and when I center myself in Spirit, I am creating an energy that influences the positive unfolding of all life. I have faith that God is bringing love and light into complete manifestation through all beings so that everyone can live in peace and harmony.

Fear to *faith*

70

We mindlessly use words all day long without realizing how truly powerful they are. Every word contains a specific energy and power, so with every word we speak or think, we create our world. The universe matches our words by giving back to us what we state; so if we want to change our experiences, a good place to start is by becoming mindful of the words we use.

I take the time today to be aware of the words I use with myself and others. I eliminate fear and anxiety by using words that are life affirming, kind and loving. My world changes when my words change.

Wouldn't our experience of life be different if we didn't feel threatened by anyone or anything? If you knew at the depth of your being that no one or nothing could harm you, how would that change your point of view? Well, the truth is that we can have this consciousness, and, yes, it requires us to go to a deep spiritual place within ourselves. When we truly believe that God is all there is and is our constant companion, we have nothing to fear.

As I experience the presence of God in all that I do and all that I am, I feel safe and secure in my world.

72

The universe always acts on our thoughts for the direction in which our life is to proceed. It is vitally important for us to be aware of what we create for ourselves. Our nature is to spiral upward, but since we have free will, sometimes we may choose to go against our nature and spiral downward in our thoughts. When the external world is unsettling, it isn't always easy to be positive. When we realize what is at stake when we choose to stay stuck in the negative, the decision to shift our consciousness is a lot easier.

I have the strength of mind to turn my focus to faith, and the flow of goodness is set free to manifest in all areas of my life.

Do you ever struggle trying to figure out who you are? I do quite often, and I always come to the conclusion that I will never be able to figure that out. I am always changing, and I am much more than the limited definitions available to describe myself. As expressions of a Divine Power both boundless and infinite, we are more than this human body and mind. We really don't need to spend our time figuring out who we are. Instead, we should just be who we are without judgment or inhibition.

I enjoy being in the flow of life, and I allow myself to be whoever I am without having to define myself. I am a unique expression of Spirit, and that is all I need to know.

74

There are times in life when my mind helps me understand my path, but there are other times when it does not. This morning things felt really complicated, and my mind was not the right instrument to use to straighten out my state of being. I decided to invite the grace of God to smooth me out. Grace is kindness, unconditional love and serenity. We are always in the presence of grace, and it is there for us to call on to make everything right within us.

Today I surrender *to the divine grace that brings me perfect peace. I don't need to figure anything out because my path unfolds through Spirit's loving direction. I am calm and relaxed as I move through my day knowing God is my guide.*

We can all take comfort in the truth that none of us knows how our lives will unfold. Life truly is a mystery. Instead of feeling powerless or scared about this we can choose to lean into God, knowing that It always shines a light for us to follow on our individual journeys. We can quiet the mind's need to know everything by trusting that Spirit guides us rightly when we listen.

Today I listen to Spirit's gentle guidance, and I can see the divine perfection of my soul's path. All is under the direction of God, so I let go of worry and concern, knowing I am exactly in the right and perfect place for all good to be made manifest.

76

This morning my mind was heavy with self-judgment. I was picking on myself for everything I saw as being "wrong" in my life. I was bullying myself. I realized this could not continue, so I took possession of my mind and started a new conversation with myself that began with the words, "You are loved."

Today I am kind and loving to myself as I embrace all that I am. Knowing that God loves me unconditionally, I follow suit and love myself unconditionally as well.

The magician is a powerful and alluring archetype in our collective consciousness. It is comforting to believe that we can reach into a magical place beyond the realm of conventional belief and produce that which we desire in our lives.

I believe we are all magicians. Through our intent and our faith, we can bring anything we desire into our lives. Spirit is the power that figures out how our desires are to manifest. We direct It through our word. As Florence Scovel Shinn said, "Your word is your wand."

Today I recognize the magician within me, and I use my magic wand, my word, to create the life of my choosing. I am grateful that Spirit figures out the details for the demonstration of my good. This is true magic.

78

Life is a dance between the human and the Divine. When the human becomes too heavy, I turn to the Divine and It lightens my load. It brings me peace and restores my soul so I can jump back into my human experience with energy and strength. It reminds me that I am a spirit having a human experience, and nothing is worth taking too seriously.

Today I rejoice in the light of God that dwells within my soul, and I move through my day with ease and grace.

Fear to *faith*

There is so much truth hidden deep within us, but we turn away from it. We are afraid of the changes we will have to make in our lives once we come face to face with the truth. None of us likes to upset our status quo, even though that status quo may be mediocre. When we muster up the courage to look at the truth we have been hiding from, the energy we have been wasting on denial is freed up. Then we can use it to create the life we have always desired.

I am filled with courage and strength *as I allow myself to see the truth. The truth cannot hurt me; it inspires and motivates me to make changes that open up the flow of goodness into my life. Spirit supports my transformation and makes my path smooth and easy.*

80

There is so much inner dialogue taking place within us at any given moment, it behooves us to pay attention to that dialogue and figure out where it is coming from — is it the head or the heart? Even though I think the heart and mind must work together, I believe the heart is the wiser voice within us because God communicates to us through our hearts. Whenever I face a decision and my mind pulls me back and forth, I put my hand on my heart and ask it for direction. This quiets my mind so I can hear my heart's guidance.

I listen to the voice of my heart knowing it guides me rightly. Spirit speaks to me through my heart, and I trust Its guidance always provides me with the perfect answers to my questions.

Fear to *faith*

In Buddhism, the cause of all suffering is said to be attachment. Attachment can take on many forms: material objects, the outcome of situations, people, etc. Letting go of our attachments is not always easy, but when we do, we take back our power. When we are attached, we create a dependency on whatever that is, and we lose sight of Spirit's ability to provide for us no matter what. When I detach, I trust that God is always supplying me with whatever it is I need to thrive.

Today I easily detach from all that causes me to suffer. I am free in the knowing that God is my eternal Source of all that I need, and my awareness of this truth allows my good to flow into my life unceasingly.

Fear to *faith*

82

Fear of death is one of our biggest fears. Imagine how different life would be if we did not have that fear. We would probably take more risks and have greater peace of mind. I have found that the more I identify with being a soul whose life goes on beyond this incarnation, the less fear I have around death.

Knowing that my soul is eternal and cannot be harmed allows me to relax into the joy of life. I see life as a great adventure, and Spirit is my guide.

Fear to *faith*

Whenever I get frustrated by what I perceive as the slow-moving wheels of justice, I remember that everything is governed by the greatest law and order that is — God. All of life is contained within the mind and body of God, and everything unfolds in a way that our little minds cannot comprehend. We all have our hands full managing our own lives; Spirit is in charge of managing the universe and balancing all that is through love and law.

Today I let go of all concerns about the world for I trust that divine justice is always unfolding in the perfect way.

Fear to *faith*

84

We should never underestimate the power of our dreams. All inventions that make our lives easier began with a dream. If your life is feeling dreary or you feel trapped by circumstances, it is time to dream — and dream big. Spirit gave us the gift of dreaming so we can grow and experience a fulfilling, joy-filled life. Dreaming is the first step for us to take if we want to change our lives.

Today I tap into my imagination and create a new dream for my life. I know that Spirit directs the unfolding of my dream, so I listen carefully to Its guidance.

_____

_____

_____

_____

_____

_____

_____

_____

_____

_____

_____

I think faith is as personal as God is to each of us. We all get our faith in different ways, but the result is the same. In the midst of uncertainty, we have the belief that everything is going to turn out well. We have past evidence that supports this belief, and so we leap over the chasm of the unknown with the awareness that something unseen is supporting us and placing us safely on the other side.

My faith in God is unshakeable, and I see Its gentle presence straightening everything out in my life. I release all worries and concerns, knowing that Spirit has it all worked out.

Fear to *faith*

86

There is absolutely no reason for us to accept negativity from others, even if it is coming from relatives, spouses or friends. We are the keepers of our boundaries, and it is our responsibility to protect ourselves from people who want to tear us down, judge us or tell us they know what is best for us. Each one of us is a temple of Spirit's love, and we must not let in anything that is contrary to our divine nature.

I am the guardian of my soul, and I do not allow anything negative to pass into my inner temple. My mind and soul are pure and clean for Spirit continually refreshes me with Its love and grace.

Fear to *faith*

Unconditional love is the greatest healing energy in the universe. Speaking for myself, and maybe some of you as well, I have mistakenly searched for it outside of myself. I can have a ton of unconditional love poured on me, but unless I have that love for myself, it won't do a bit of good. Loving ourselves is not arrogant or selfish — it is vital for our well-being. If we cannot love ourselves, then we have work to do.

Today I give myself unconditional love as I bask in the light of the divine energy of Spirit that dwells within me. I appreciate who I am and how I show up in this world as the presence of love.

Fear to *faith*

88

Nourishment takes place on many levels for us, and we choose what is going to enter into our body, mind and soul for that nourishment. We decide what food to give our body, what ideas and information to feed our mind, and which people to feed us with support and love. Every now and then, it is good to examine what we are feeding ourselves since there is so much junk food, junk ideas and information and, dare I say, junk people in the world. We are the only ones responsible for what enters into our body, mind and soul, so let's make life-enhancing choices so we can live a healthy life.

Today I am mindful of the food I eat, the information I expose myself to and the people I engage with, and I choose only that which is good for me. I nourish myself with the healthiest of everything, and I experience a vibrant, energized life.

Fear to *faith*

Even though we may feel separated from Spirit because we cannot understand why certain things are happening in our lives, the truth is that God is always present regardless of what we think. The only thing that separates us from God is our consciousness. Shame, anger, fear and resentment are the bricks in the wall that we build in our minds that prevent us from connecting to God. On the other side of the wall is the light of Spirit, which is always ready and willing to fill us up with faith and love.

Today I tear down the wall that separates me from God, and It pours Its light and love into me. All is healed.

90

Wanting to go back to another time in our lives is a natural inclination, especially if we are uncomfortable with where we are. Rather than looking backward for relief from our discomfort, this feeling is a call for us to look more closely at what is before us. Even if something is not going right or not as we planned, there certainly is something good that we are overlooking. At any given moment, there are at least 10 things we can be grateful for. Going backward creates denial; focusing on the present and what is good brings joy.

Today I am able see the bountiful good that is in my life, and I am grateful for the multitude of blessings Spirit has bestowed upon me. The present truly is a present from God.

Yesterday after services, a man fell down right in front of me as I was walking toward him. It was clear I would not be able to stop him from falling, so I stretched out my arms underneath him in an effort to cushion his fall. Someone came over to help him get up, but the man was fragile, and told us he needed to pull himself up because if we pulled him up, it could hurt him. He just needed us for support as he stood up.

As I look back on this experience, I see a great lesson. When people fall down in life, it is our natural instinct to want to pull them up immediately so they can get back on their feet as soon as possible. However, we cannot force ourselves on anyone when they are rising from a fall; we need to allow them to get up in a way that is comfortable for them. Our part is just to be a supportive presence.

I give all beings the space to rise up in their own way. I know there is an Inner Knower nestled within all people that gives them the direction to get back on their feet again.

92

The human mind does not like to be in a state of unknowing. I see this in myself when I am going through an experience, and I want to know how it is going to turn out. My mind will begin contemplating various scenarios, and before I know it, I am all worked up. When this happens, I stop the storytelling and remind myself that I don't need to know how the situation is going to turn out. I surrender to the mystery, and trust that everything is unfolding through Spirit's guidance. I leave it alone.

I let go of the need to know *how everything in my life is going to unfold for I trust that God guides the outcome of all that is. I relax into this truth, and I am free.*

Fear to *faith*

All of us at times face life situations in serious need of change. It can be really frustrating trying to figure out what those changes need to be. We can stare at the problem and summon all of our mental energy to help us, yet no solutions come forward. One strategy I have found to be effective is to look at the situation from a different angle. I can do this by asking myself how someone I respect might look at the situation. By engaging my imagination, my perspective shifts to a different way of viewing the situation, allowing me to see the perfect solution.

Today I look at my life situations from a different viewpoint, *and all the answers I have been seeking come pouring into my consciousness.*

94

Everything we give our attention to becomes a part of us. We drink it in, digest it and absorb it. I know there is a lot I give my attention to that does not make me feel good, especially in regards to the strife that is present in our world today. My solution is to drink from the well of Spirit, and drink often. It purifies all the toxic energy that is rampant in our world that I may have taken in, and It releases it from my heart. This allows me to be in this world but not embody the negative and be hurt by it.

Today I drink from the inexhaustible well of Spirit, and my soul is cleansed and rejuvenated. My energy is fresh and vibrant, as I experience life with new eyes.

Fear to *faith*

Every day, we awaken to a blank canvas that is ours to use to create the day of our choosing. We are the artists of our lives, and our choices are the paint that form the picture of our experience. Spirit has given us an infinite palette of colors to use to create our day. All we have to do is rise above limitation and plug into the vast array of possibilities that lie within us.

I acknowledge the artist within me as I create a day that is filled with color, love and boundless joy. Spirit has given me a blank canvas to paint the life of my choosing.

Fear to *faith*

96

I am fascinated by our culture's obsession with looking younger. In an effort to recapture our lost youth, we spend an incredible amount of time and money changing how we look on the outside. If we truly want to turn back the hands of time, our work must be focused inward. The distance that is created between youth and wherever we are now can be collapsed in a heartbeat by realizing that feeling young is a state of mind we can access at any moment. When we release the burdens, worries and heaviness that result from living life and connect with our ageless spirit, then we have found the fountain of youth.

I tap into the vibrant youthful place in my soul, and I am rejuvenated. My heart is made young again, as I see life through fresh eyes.

_____

_____

_____

_____

_____

_____

_____

Fear to *faith* _____

There is a lot going on in our world right now that can cause us to harden our hearts. There is so much that does not make sense; so much that seems unnecessary; so much that appears backwards and un-evolved. In our journey through this time, it serves us well to exercise compassion. As challenging as it may be, living with a hard heart toward anyone or anything is not good for us. We don't need to accept that which is disturbing in the world, but if we can soften our hearts and understand that what we are seeing is just the result of unhealed past trauma, then we contribute to the healing of the trauma through our consciousness. The divine harmony of Spirit heals everything in our world, even though it isn't completely evident yet.

Today I soften my heart and trust that Spirit is bringing healing to the entire world.

98

Everyone has an inner judge. Its purpose is to give us the ability to discern so we can make good choices in life. However, if not kept in check, the judge can create inner turmoil, especially if we are harshly critical of ourselves or others. I know that when my inner judge is out of control, I don't feel very good, whether I am judging myself or others. I have found that turning to God's unconditional love silences my inner judge. Love collapses the separation judgment creates and restores our consciousness to wholeness, allowing us to feel oneness with God and all life.

I embrace the unconditional love of Spirit, and all judgment and feelings of separation disappear from my heart and mind. I am at peace knowing we are all doing the best we can in this life.

Fear to *faith*

Being the creators of our lives, sometimes we have to erase the plans we drew up and start over. Starting over can elicit feelings of wasted time or frustration, but in reality, starting over is part of the creative process. Just because a plan did not work out doesn't mean it didn't have a purpose. That aborted plan paved the way for a better plan to emerge. Every idea serves a purpose in our lives whether it worked or not.

I allow myself to discard any plans I made that are not working for me, and I open up to a better idea from Spirit.

Fear to *faith*

100

Many of us have had to figure out how life works on our own. One of the greatest lessons I have learned and continue to learn is that I don't have to force things to happen. After I do my inner work and open up to a new path, the next step is to move my consciousness to a higher view so I can clearly see the possibilities and opportunities being revealed to me. I don't have to make things happen; I just have to glide in the field of infinite possibilities and pursue whatever catches my eye as mine do to.

As I soar in Spirit's energy, I keep my eyes open to the opportunities that come my way that move me forward on my journey.

Fear to faith

Living a mindful spiritual life oftentimes requires us to pass through narrow passage-ways to overcome old ways of thinking. Yes-terday I had an experience in which I had to walk through that sort of passageway. Something insignificant happened, but the experience was enough to awaken an old belief that tells me I am a failure. I was present to what was going on in my consciousness as I delicately loosened my attachment to this old belief. I felt like I was walking through a narrow passageway. I knew if I stopped being aware of what was happening within my mind, the waters of the old belief would engulf me. However, I gingerly made my way through the passage-way, and I came out on the other side with my self-esteem fully intact.

As I navigate through my life experiences, I know that Spirit guides me through the narrow passageways with love and wisdom so that I can conquer old beliefs and rise up triumphant in my true self.

102

It is so important for us to acknowledge and celebrate the small victories we experience every day. We can get so fixated on whatever it is we want changed or healed in our life that we forget that the path to change consists of small victories. Whether we are walking through a health issue, financial recovery or a broken relationship, every step we take contains triumph. When we recognize that, we accelerate the completion of our healing.

Today I celebrate the small victories that lead me to my complete healing. As I recognize the triumphs I make every single day, I open the door to my good to come pouring into my life.

Fear to *faith*

The word "paradise" conjures up such delightful feelings and mental imagery. The idea of awe-inspiring natural beauty, soothing peace, splendor and absolute perfection is tantalizing. And God knows, we need to escape to some sort of paradise every now and then to balance out the challenges of life.

As wonderful as eternally living in paradise may sound, we humans have spiritual work to do, and that requires us to be present in this world of contrast. Spirit has given us the strength and resiliency to walk through any experience, and It has also given us the ability to summon up paradise within our own minds. In the midst of any challenge, by recognizing our many blessings and seeing the presence of Spirit in our lives, we can bring paradise into our consciousness whenever we like.

I am grateful God has given me unlimited power and strength to walk through any experience, as well as the ability to see that paradise lies within me.

It is natural for us to grow and expand ourselves; it is not natural for us to shrink and contract. Deep within every person is a longing to be more than we are in this present moment. There is unexplored territory within us that is yearning to be tapped into so we can bring our deepest passions into expression. It is the unique essence of who we are that is ready to emerge. We may ignore it because we fear its power. We may ignore it because it might cause us to make changes to our life. However, we pay a high price when we do not listen to the calling of our soul.

I pay attention to the inner longings of my soul, and I take action that brings these longings into expression. I know that Spirit is the driving force behind my deepest soul yearnings, so I honor the Divine within me.

Waiting does not receive the value it rightly deserves. In this impatient world we live in, no one wants to wait; we want everything right now. However, when it comes to making important life decisions or responding to something that triggered us, waiting serves us well. Something unsettling was revealed in a group I am a member of, and we all jumped into the "we have to do something right now" mindset. After spending a little time in that energy, we all realized that we need to relax and take our time finding just the right solution.

I honor the time I need to make good decisions in my life, knowing that Spirit reveals the answers I am seeking in the perfect way and time.

106

Nestled within all of us is an inner knowing that provides us with peace, comfort and the assurance that all is well. This inner knowing is not influenced by outer circumstances, nor is it controlled by our conscious thought. This knowing is our higher wisdom that comes from Spirit, and it can be called upon 24/7. Whenever I get affected by the passage of time, global instability or anything fearful, I still my mind and connect with my higher wisdom. It reminds me that there is a part of me that is forever whole and untouched by anything that is of this world.

I plug into my inner wisdom, and all fear disappears as I remember the spiritual truth of who I am. I know there is a higher level of seeing life that brings me comfort. I invite that truth to penetrate my mind, and I am at peace.

The other day I was talking with a friend in the sanctuary of the spiritual center I serve, and during our conversation, I said to him, "This is a house of God." He put his hand on his heart and said, "So is this." I was speechless; he was so right. Each one of us is a house in which Spirit dwells, and we don't need to go anywhere to connect with It, because It lives within us.

I recognize I am a house in which God dwells, and no matter what I am experiencing, Spirit is always at the center of my being.

108

Recently, I have been contemplating how to balance living in the here and now while thinking about where I want to go in the future. I was really struggling trying to understand how the two can coexist. How can I be living in the here and now if I am thinking about where I want my life to go? Then I realized that time is fluid. Past, present and future all exist at the same time. So in truth, I am never fixed in any one station of time; it is only my consciousness that anchors me into a certain time and space. I realized that while it is necessary for me to focus my attention on creating my future, when I am finished putting enough energy on that, I can shift my attention to being present to where I am in the here and now.

I recognize that time is a human construct, so I use my consciousness to create a future that is fulfilling while enjoying and appreciating what is presently in my world.

It is true that we are all the directors of our lives. We set up the shots, write the story and choose the actors. It is amazing that with all these movies going on simultaneously in the world, we are able to function as well as we do.

I know a lot of people who are going through serious challenges right now, and they are intensely focused on the problems they are experiencing. Using the movie analogy, this is the perfect time for the camera to pull into a wide shot so the full picture can be seen. Rather than intensely focusing on the issue, look farther out and see what possibilities are contained within the frame that cannot be seen when the focus is fixed on the problem.

I widen my focus so that I can see all the possibilities that exist for the solution to any challenges I may be experiencing. Spirit always provides me with the perfect ideas when I expand my vision to see them.

110

The first step to changing our lives is to change ourselves. We can't continue being the same person we have always been and expect our lives to be anything different. I am walking through this experience right now. I have found that some things I have been doing in my life no longer suit me for I have outgrown them. My work is cut out for me. I have to figure out what new things I would like to do and change my beliefs about who I am and what I am capable of doing so I can grow into a new me and a new life.

I courageously embrace the process of transformation, knowing that Spirit supports me through all the inner changes that bring about the new life I am ready to experience.

Fear to *faith*

No matter how much healing and re-leasing we have done in regards to our past, we cannot deny our roots. Who we are today is connected to where we came from. Once the pain of the past is healed, we can appreciate the transformation we achieved and acknowledge our power and strength. We can see how ugly experiences turned into the beauty of who we are today. When you look at the roots of any vegetation, they aren't aesthetically pleasing; however, the tree, plant or flower those roots support is most beautiful. Just like us.

I appreciate my roots for they support the person I am today. I honor my past and have learned well from it, as I rise up and continue growing through God's grace.

I was having a conversation with someone, and she was telling me how everything went wrong for her in the morning; it was one thing after another. When she was done telling me her tale of woe, I said, "This stops now. All the chaos that took place this morning is done, and now everything is flowing smoothly."

I was reminded how I used to allow morning disruptions to set the tone for my day. If a few things went awry, I would assume that the whole day was going to be out of control. What was I thinking? Maybe you have said to yourself on occasion after a similar experience, "This is going to be one of those days." We totally set ourselves up for more negativity when we make statements like that.

The truth is that any trajectory of energy can be interrupted by our consciousness. We have all the power necessary to set new energy in motion through our belief and intention. We don't need to affirm that our whole day is going to be chaotic just because it starts out that way.

I use my consciousness to create the day I would like to experience today. I no longer allow circumstances to control the energy of my day; instead, I set my intention to bring forth a day of peace and joy.

Fear to *faith*

Even though I am well beyond my teenage years, there is a teenager who still lives within me, and she recently took over my consciousness. She is rebellious, stubborn and sassy — and it has been interesting watching her wreak havoc in my mind. As much as I aspire to keep my consciousness in a high place, my inner teenager pulled me into a lower strata of thinking. Rather than shaming myself because I wasn't feeling very evolved, I stopped judging and resisting her. I decided to pay attention to my inner teenager and connect with her, because she was clearly trying to get my attention and tell me something I needed to hear.

Her message to me was that there was something I was accepting in my life that I didn't need to accept anymore. She, being the wise rebel she is, came out to tell me that there comes a time when we have to say "no" and be ok with that.

I honor the different parts of myself as messengers of truth. When a part of me is trying to get my attention, I listen so that I can grow and move forward in my life. It is just another way Spirit speaks to me.

Recently, I met with a new women's group I just started. As we were introducing ourselves to each other and talking about our lives, I noticed how each woman is a book that is in the process of being written. One of the commonalities we share is that all of us are ready for some sort of movement forward in our own personal journey. Some of us are ready to start a new chapter, and some are right in the middle of a chapter.

As I reflect on this, I am present to the discomfort of yearning for a shift whose time has not yet come. Being in the company of others who are experiencing the same thing brings great peace. It reminds me that when we come together to share such experiences of the heart, we loosen up stagnant energy, which in turn facilitates our desired shifts.

I see my life as a book I am forever writing, and even though I may not know how it will unfold, I have faith that Spirit is guiding me through each chapter so that I can create a fulfilling and meaningful life.

Fear to faith

There is a lush, beautiful world all of us can visit any time we choose. You don't have to book a reservation to visit this place because it is within you. There is no judgment or fear in this world because it is pure, undiluted Spiritual energy. We can visit this place through meditation, prayer or visualization.

I love to go to this sacred zone every day to remind myself of what is true and real. I am able to strip away feelings of doubt, alienation and fear because I connect with God in this place. I am cleansed of all that is not in harmony with my Divine Self when I go to this world. When I leave this place, I always bring something back with me, whether it is a word, an idea or just a feeling that reminds me to think of this world as I am experiencing my day.

Within me lies the beautiful, loving world of Spirit, and I go there often to refresh my soul and remind myself that I am a divine expression of all that God is. My heart is lifted as I bring back the light of Spirit into my world.

116

Every now and then we reach the point when we have to give up on something we have been putting a lot of energy into because it just isn't working. It can be difficult to admit this to ourselves, but it is also liberating. We should not feel shame if we have exhausted all resources and ideas and cannot figure out how to make something work. Oftentimes surrendering opens the space for new ideas to emerge because we release the pressure within ourselves, which loosens up our creativity.

I trust myself to know when to surrender that which I cannot figure out. If something is not working, I let it go and Spirit guides me in a new direction that brings forth my good.

Fear to *faith*

Self-trust doesn't always come easy. When we feel insecure about making the right decision, it is only natural to seek advice or guidance from someone who is an expert. What do we do if that advice does not seem right for us to follow? Do we blindly follow it because the expert told us to? What if our heart is screaming at us not to follow their advice? Do we override our instincts?

My advice is to never doubt yourself. Even in the midst of expert opinions, we ultimately know what is best for us. There is an Intelligence greater than all human minds put together that knows the right path for us to follow, and It lives within our hearts. That is the expert to listen to.

I trust that the guiding power of Spirit within me always leads me to make the right decisions.

_____

_____

_____

_____

_____

_____

_____

Fear to *faith*

118

Sometimes in this life we get bombarded with non-stop situations and circumstances that elicit fear, and it feels impossible to get free of the anxiety. Working with the mind by using spiritual truth is a great way to generate inner peace in the midst of fear and uncertainty. When I take my attention off the transitory nature of life and focus my consciousness on Spirit and the eternal essence of my being, instead of identifying with circumstances that are always in flux and out of my control, my peace is restored.

I identify with the Source of life that is immune to the fluctuations and changes of the human world, and I draw the peace of Spirit into my heart so that I can relax and move through life with ease.

Fear to *faith*

It is only human to build a fortress around ourselves for protection when we get hurt in life. The problem with that is we shut ourselves off from letting new experiences and people into our lives. The truth is we don't need to hide behind anything to protect ourselves from hurt. When we have a painful experience, we heal through understanding, compassion and wisdom — not by putting up a barrier between ourselves and life. We learn from our experiences, and that is our protection. We are here to fully engage in life and experience all this world has to offer.

My spirit is strong and resilient, and I welcome new experiences into my life that expand my heart and soul. Spirit guides me rightly so that my choices are always in my highest and best good.

120

Recently, a dear sweet soul I had the honor to know made his transition. This was one of those situations where nothing made sense. He was young, healthy and full of life. No one could understand why he fell ill and passed so quickly.

We see this story play out all the time. The mind cannot grasp why tragic things happen when there is no warning. What I have come to know is that there are things in life that appear to come out of nowhere, and I just have to give my mind time to adjust to what is occurring. Even though every fiber of my being wants to stop what is happening and fix it, there is something bigger unfolding that I have to accept.

And of course, I must turn to Spirit and invite Its love and peace in to calm my soul.

I let go of the need to understand and control that which is beyond my understanding. As I recognize there is a greater wisdom that directs all life, my mind is filled with peace knowing all is well.

_____

_____

_____

_____

Fear to *faith*

I know that so many of us are great at serving others. When someone is in need, you are right there. Are you as adept at receiving as you are at giving? We live in a universe that eternally asks us, "How may I serve you?" What is your answer? Do you say, "No thank you," or do you place your order without holding anything back? Giving and receiving are two sides of the same spiritual law, and in order to have a balanced and fulfilled life, we must give and receive in equal measure.

Knowing that the universe gives generously to all beings, I open up to receive my good, and I circulate that good to others.

122

Yesterday I reversed a decision I made because I realized it was not healthy for me. However, the reversal disappointed someone. I struggled with fear and shame because I thought my change of heart compromised my integrity. Then I had an epiphany this morning when I remembered it is ok to change my mind. Wow! Changing my mind has nothing to do with my integrity; I am actually taking care of myself when I change my mind.

Knowing that life is ever changing, I follow my heart and change my direction whenever I feel it is necessary. I give myself permission to change my mind if I know it is the right thing for me to do.

Fear to *faith*

Darkness gets a bad rap. I read something this morning that said that darkness generates energy for change, and it also contains the formless space from which we create. Darkness is part of the human experience for a reason. I can speak for myself and many of you when I say that even though we have walked through a lot of darkness in our lives, we came out on the other side and into the light to start fresh again. When we are going through a dark period, we shouldn't fight it but learn from it and recognize that it is a catalyst for positive change.

I see the good that darkness brings into my life knowing that God always leads me back into the light. I honor all aspects of this human experience as my evolution unfolds with grace and ease.

_____

_____

_____

_____

_____

_____

_____

124

Recently, I started working with a personal trainer because I needed someone to hold me accountable for meeting my fitness goals. When I was leaving the house yesterday to go work out, I was mindful of my inner chatter. As I opened the door to leave and felt the oppressive humidity, my immediate reaction was, "I can't do this. All the energy just left my body." I really wanted to walk back into my home and just lounge. But I had made a commitment to myself, so I overrode my mind and had a great workout.

This experience reminded me how important discipline is to reaching our goals. Whenever we want to make big changes to ourselves or to our lives, we have to change something about our behavior, and that isn't always comfortable or easy. However, the end results are wonderful. We just have to hook into our commitment and discipline so we can be pulled into the action that allows us to achieve our goals.

As I recognize I have all the support of the universe behind me, I am able to do anything I set my mind to do. I have the power to create new habits that allow me to reach all my personal goals.

_____

_____

_____

Fear to *faith*

Those of us walking on the spiritual path like to expose ourselves to a lot of truth. We read books, take classes, read inspirational quotes on Facebook and Instagram, etc. However, the real work comes when we focus on just one truth, take it into our hearts and contemplate what that truth means to us and how we can embody it.

Recently, I had that opportunity. As I was looking at a group of people sitting across from me at breakfast, I thought about how my history, education and judgments were influencing what I was seeing. I asked myself how I could purify my mind and see without categorizing, assuming or projecting. The answer I got was to look through different eyes — to look through God's eyes.

This is a challenging practice, but it brings great inner peace. When we become aware of the distortions of our own perceptions, we clear the way for Spirit's eyes to become our eyes.

As I deepen my awareness of my subjective perceptions, I detach from them and open myself up to Spirit's vision that sees all as light and love.

Fear to *faith*

126

Every major life experience we have moves us into a new world requiring us to make adjustments to how we are going to live our lives under new conditions. When the rug feels as though it has been pulled out from underneath us, we must get up slowly and reorient ourselves rather than frantically trying to get up and figure out how we are going to restore our equilibrium. When I experience a life jolt, part of me wants to urgently reinstate some sort of normalcy and balance, but there is another part of me that knows better. I have to give myself time to adjust because I need to figure out the landscape of the new world I am living in. The good news is that order and balance always emerge in time, so I lean into Spirit's comfort and grace until it does.

God has given me the ability to adjust to any new world I may find myself in. I give myself time to regain my balance, knowing that Spirit is right where I am.

_____

_____

_____

_____

_____

_____

Fear to *faith*

For many years, I was a doormat. I allowed people to walk all over me as I turned a deaf ear to my heart. I did not stand up for myself because my self-esteem was nonexistent. I am happy to say that those days are over. However, there are moments when I find myself in situations when I need to stop and check in with myself and see if it is really healthy and right for me to give to another or if I am just doing so to please the other person. Sometimes giving of the self requires a little review before acting.

My heart always guides me rightly, for I know there are times when I have to say no. Spirit has given me the gift of discretion, and it serves me well.

128

Each one of us is the captain of our own ship. We make all the decisions about the course of our life's direction. We navigate through every experience and steer our journey through this sea of life. Sometimes I like to go to a beautiful island and rest. Other times I seek a bigger adventure, and I set sail into unknown territory and stormy seas. The cool thing is that this is my ship, my life, and I am the captain.

Every now and then I have to remind myself of this truth when I mistakenly think forces outside of me control my fate. I have all the power to create my own map, pull up anchor and sail to a new land. I know that wherever my journey leads me, everything always turns out well because my compass is always pointed toward Spirit.

I am the captain of my life, and I delight in the freedom Spirit has given me to sail my ship wherever I choose. Life is an adventure of the soul, and I take my direction from God.

One of the most challenging of human experiences is dealing with emptiness. Our impulse is to immediately fill up the void with something so that we don't have to feel the loss of that which is no longer in our life. However, this can result in making a poor choice since we are coming from a place of desperation.

The best strategy for dealing with emptiness is not to run away from it or try to quickly fill it up. If we face it head on, we can see it for what it is — a transitory experience. Everything comes and goes on this plane of existence; the cycle never ends. So if we experience emptiness, we can trust that something new is coming into our life, but we must honor our process of fully letting go of the old so that the new can come in.

In the midst of emptiness, I am filled up by the presence of Spirit as It restores me to wholeness.

Fear to *faith*

130

One of the qualities of being human is that we love to fill empty space. Whether it is physical space or the space of not knowing, when we encounter it, we begin to fill it up. A friend of mine has the spiritual practice of saying to herself first thing upon waking, "I know nothing." This is a great way to start the day with a clear and open mind.

We make a lot of assumptions throughout our waking hours in order to fill the gaps of not knowing, even though our assumptions may not be correct. By beginning our day with the understanding that we don't know it all, we can enter our day with a clear and open mind and experience deep inner peace.

As I let go of the need to think I know everything, I am able to objectively see the world around me without projecting my thoughts upon it.

Whenever we have a problem that needs to be solved or an inner disturbance that needs to be worked out, most of us immediately go to our brain to get answers and direction. And why not? The brain is a marvelous device for us to use. However, sometimes the brain doesn't guide us rightly, especially if we are going in circles and not arriving at peace. I recently discovered a wonderful new tool to use when this happens. I visualize taking the issue away from my brain and giving it to my heart to ponder. Then I thank my brain for trying to help, and I listen to my heart's point of view.

My heart always guides me rightly for all the wisdom of the universe is housed there. It provides me with all the answers that create freedom, joy and abundance in my life.

132

One of the greatest gifts we can give to another person is to listen to them without interrupting. We have been so conditioned to react and give immediate feedback when we are in conversation with people that we have forgotten the value of simply listening without having to insert ourselves. Too many people feel invisible because they don't feel heard. If we can be present to others and give them space to speak and be sincerely listened to, we are deeply honoring them and raising them up without saying a word.

I listen to others with an open heart *and a closed mouth, knowing I am validating them by being a witness to their experience.*

In some spiritual belief systems, there is an emphasis on detaching from our desires and living a life of simplicity and neutrality. In my personal spiritual belief system, even though I advocate non-attachment and keeping a healthy attitude toward things and people, I think we should honor our desires. This morning I purposely asked myself what it is I am thirsting for in my life. Sometimes I need to knock on my heart's door and ask what it is yearning for, and it loves to tell me.

What are you thirsting for? If you don't ask the question, the universe can't deliver it to you.

I open up to my soul's deepest yearnings, and I activate the universal energy that creates the path for those yearnings to be realized.

134

In ancient times, a solar eclipse evoked fear in people. In some cultures it was seen as a bad omen; in others there was fear that the sun was being extinguished. Today it is simply a natural phenomenon that brings excitement and joy to many.

It is human nature to jump to conclusions based on what is appearing in our world. When the ancient cultures saw the sun being eclipsed by the moon, they assumed the worst. We still have that propensity within us. Instead of assuming the worst when we have a personal eclipse in our life and experience darkness, if we stay present and remember that the sun is coming back out, we can remain in peace no matter what.

Today I see my life as a reflection of all the amazing celestial events that appear in this world, knowing that my light can never be extinguished.

_____

_____

_____

_____

_____

_____

_____

Fear to *faith*

I felt stagnant yesterday, so I turned to one of my favorite authors, Raymond Charles Barker, for help. As Spirit would have it, I opened up to a passage about circulation. Barker says that to keep our lives flowing and vibrant, we must make sure we are circulating our energy in all forms: love, money, things, etc. As I pondered what I read, my first thought was to clean out a drawer or a closet and circulate things I no longer need. The more I thought about that, I realized that wasn't the answer. The answer is bigger than circulating things; it is about having open circulation in all areas of life.

We live on four planes of existence — mental, physical, emotional and spiritual — and each area must have unrestricted circulation. So our task is to figure out which areas of our lives are not circulating energy and loosen that energy so that we can reinstate the unobstructed flow of life.

I open up all channels of expression and release any stagnant energy that may be interfering with the divine circulation of my soul.

136

It is human nature to want to give direction to people who we think are doing something wrong, unhealthy or misguided in their lives. The truth is that it is none of our business unless they ask us for advice. The only person we are responsible for is ourselves, and there is plenty of work for us to do to heal our own stuff. We must tend to our own issues rather than focusing on everyone else's. Whenever I notice that I am judging someone in this way, I turn it on myself and ask what this judgment is telling me about myself so that I can do the inner work that brings me freedom.

I take full responsibility for the upkeep of my being as I honor others on their individual paths. Spirit continually reveals all I need to know to improve myself and my life experience.

Fear to *faith*

We don't give ourselves enough credit for the effort it takes to do this thing called life every day. The amount of mental and emotional energy it takes just to manage our identity is enormous. One of my favorite aspects of being on the spiritual path is knowing there is a Higher Power that I can surrender to and relax my whole being into at any time, and I can let go of needing to figure myself out. I love giving myself a break from managing who I am and just let God be God in, as and through me, so I can relax and enjoy this life as it was meant to be enjoyed.

I let go of the need to manage my identity *today, and I relax in being the unique divine expression of Spirit that I am.*

138

Underneath the layers of our humanity lies our soul — the pure essence of who we truly are, and it sits upon a throne that is in the center of our beingness. This throne is charged with the energy of God, and it is made of love and peace. We have the choice of running our entire life from this vantage point or not.

As we experience life, we may forget about the seat of the soul and the holy throne that we sit on. When we feel lost and afraid, we truly have forgotten where our soul resides. We are the kings and queens of our lives, and we are the only ones who control ourselves and how we react to life. It is time for us to take our rightful place on our thrones and rule our lives from a place of spiritual insight.

I claim the throne of my soul and govern my life rooted in my spiritual power.

Fear to *faith*

The quest for inner peace oftentimes requires us to examine our mental habits so we can become aware of those that create discord within us. This can cause a great deal of resistance because we are attached to our mental habits and see them as necessary for our functioning in this world.

One mental habit that falls into this category is being opinionated. Have you ever thought what it would be like to spend a day without having an opinion about anything and just be neutral? My challenge for all of us today is to become aware of how often our minds are issuing an opinion about something and how that makes us feel on the inside. If your answer is not, "It makes me feel at peace," then it is time to break that habit.

I let go of the need to have an opinion about anything, and my mind relaxes in the flow of peace that is my true nature.

140

Like many of you, I was raised to think it was not good to be messy. My mom was a total neat freak. If I accidentally spilled something, she went into a frenzy. I think in the depths of my psyche I translated this to believing that the path of life was also supposed to be neat and orderly.

Decades later, when I was introduced to the concept that it is normal for life to be messy, I was so relieved. All of our lives are disorderly and confusing at times, but Divine Order is always working in the background to help us clean up the mess and bring everything into a new pattern of life. I have learned to see there is good in the mess.

I recognize that even though life can be messy, it is part of the cycle of creating new good in my life. Spirit always guides me to transform all my messes into something new and wonderful.

Life is continually pulling us to explore new territory, whether it is outside of us or within us. This is a good thing, otherwise we would be stagnant and never grow. There are so many unexplored experiences for us to venture into. Living in a small, predictable world only limits us from expanding our lives and our consciousness.

Sometimes we are forced to explore this territory; sometimes it is our choice. No matter what the cause, we have the power to create an amazing new life experience for ourselves by setting our intention to be intuitively guided by Spirit to the perfect places for us to meet our good and have an abundance of it. Whatever new territory we find ourselves walking into, there is no place for fear — only faith.

I greet new experiences with enthusiasm and faith, knowing God walks with me wherever I go.

142

One of the most challenging questions I am asked is how to cultivate faith. Faith is not something that can be taught. It is extremely personal and something that naturally evolves by connecting to the God of our understanding.

What I know about faith is that it cannot be based on our personal expectations being met. That is one of the biggest destroyers of faith. Faith must be based on the understanding that we live in a spiritual universe that is governed by love and law — and that our good is continually unfolding through Spirit's direction. When we hook our faith into that truth, we see God in action without our having to control how that good shows up in our lives.

As I deepen my connection to Spirit, my faith grows exponentially. I see God's handiwork in all areas of my life, and I am at peace.

It is no secret that I am all about enlisting the power of Spirit to help us in every aspect of our lives. Opening up the divine portal of our consciousness and inviting God in to straighten everything out activates a course of action that guides us rightly and creates mind-blowing synchronicity. Rather than staying stuck in what appears to be unsolvable problems, all we need to do is say, "I'm giving this up to Spirit to straighten out. Where there is illness, Spirit reveals health. Where there is lack, Spirit reveals abundance. Where there is confusion, Spirit reveals clarity."

Today I invite the presence of Spirit into my life to right everything that appears to be wrong, and the results are astounding. Thank you, God!

144

Walking the spiritual path can get heavy and serious at times. Knowing in our hearts the good that humanity is capable of demonstrating and not seeing it can dampen our spirits. There are many solutions to this inner dilemma: pray, meditate, get involved, etc.

However, I have one more idea to add to the list: laugh. We have to remember not to take this world too seriously. Life is transitory, and we were not created to live in heaviness. Even though there are unsettling things that happen in life and in the world at large, we must lighten up and know that the universe is a place of law and order. Goodness and love always triumph.

I lighten my heart and see the humor in life. I allow myself to laugh out loud throughout the day and feel the joy that lives within me.

Watching Superman as a child, I was always fascinated by the power Kryptonite had over him. How this beautiful green stone could cripple the "Man of Steel" was mind-boggling. We can turn this into a personal spiritual lesson because we all have our own forms of Kryptonite that weaken us. There are certain situations, people or things that cripple us at the very thought of them.

Rather than staying frozen in a state of helplessness, we can break the spell of the Kryptonite and take our power back. We have the ability to eliminate the authority we have given to our own personal Kryptonite by realizing that it isn't the Kryptonite itself that weakens us but rather our belief that it can.

I take back the power *I have given to anyone or anything that weakens me, and my wholeness in reinstated. The power of Spirit provides me with the strength to stand strong in all that I encounter in my life.*

Fear to *faith*

146

Being the human that I am, there are times when I feel like the universe is not listening to me. I can pray, know, affirm and declare — and still nothing. In my practitioner training, I was taught that if I am not demonstrating what I desire, there is only one place to look — within. It truly is done unto us as we believe, so if something isn't happening, then I don't believe it can. Even though I may think I am ready to receive, if I am not receiving, then there is a hidden doubt that needs to be unearthed.

It isn't easy to dig up those blocks, but it can be done. Just ask Spirit to reveal them, and they will be revealed.

I clear my inner space of all doubts that block my good. I confidently tell the universe what I am ready to receive, and I receive abundantly.

When we second-guess ourselves, we disconnect from the inexhaustible well of inner knowledge that sustains us and guides us rightly. We all know what is right for us. If we think things through and check in with our intuition, our decisions come from a solid place, and there is no need to second-guess ourselves.

In truth, life is a grand experiment, and there are no perfect answers. We do the best we can each step of the way and have faith that our inner guidance system takes us in the right direction. Good comes out of everything, so we can never go wrong.

I trust my decisions *knowing I am always guided rightly to do what is best wherever I am in my life experience. Spirit is the unquenchable light that forever directs me along my beautiful path.*

148

When I awoke this morning, the most interesting question crossed my mind: Why am I not starting each day telling my mind how it can serve me and what I expect from it? Why do I just wait and see where it is going to take me and then reel it in depending on its reactions? Doesn't it make sense to put our minds in their right and proper place so that we are its master rather than it mastering us?

Here is something we can say to our minds to set up that relationship each day. "Good morning, mind! I expect you to be calm in the face of uncertainty and comfortable not knowing everything or how things are going to turn out. I expect you to be present to what is before us and not look back to old patterns for comfort. I expect you to serve me in the highest way possible by deferring to Spirit for all direction."

Today I remember that I am the master of my consciousness, and I use the power of my intention to create my experience of life.

Fear to *faith*

One of the wonderful things about this
time we live in is the abundance of spiritual
wisdom that is right at our fingertips. There is
such a wide variety of ideas for us to consider about
the life of the soul. However, sometimes I get so overwhelmed by it all that I don't know who is right.

That is when I put all the books down, shut off the
internet, put my hand over my heart, and return to the
simplicity of the great I Am. I remind myself that all
I need to know about spirituality lies within my sacred
heart: God is, I am, and love is always the answer.

*Today, I see how very simple it is to live in the light of Spirit.
I still my mind, open my heart and invite the Divine Presence
to fill me up with peace and love.*

150

One of my biggest life lessons I am still mastering is standing up and speaking my truth when people in authority are incorrect. There is still a little girl inside of me who thinks you shouldn't question people in authority.

As Spirit would have it, last week I was presented with an opportunity to once again attempt to master this lesson. Someone I know who is in a leadership position spoke as if he were an authority on something, and he was clearly untrained in what he was doing. At first I thought I wouldn't say anything, but at 3:00 this morning, my inner tigress woke me up and told me I needed to speak my truth. And so I did, and now I feel much better.

I trust myself to speak my truth whenever I see fit. I am safe in expressing anything I need to say, for Spirit is always with me.

Fear to faith

When fear grabs our attention, love disappears. It is said that we cannot feel both love and fear at the same time, so the solution to letting go of fear is to center ourselves in love. Deep within all of us is an inexhaustible reservoir of love that we can drink from at any time. We just need to completely turn our focus toward love and let it fill us up and dissolve any fear we may be experiencing.

Love truly is the greatest healing power there is.

I live my life immersed in and surrounded by Spirit's love. It restores my inner peace and brings balance to my life.

152

I always pay attention to things that cross my path more than once in a day. Yesterday two different people spoke to me about peacocks, so I knew I needed to research what that might mean. My research clarified that the peacock symbolizes vision, royalty, spirituality, awakening, guidance, protection and watchfulness. What a perfect symbol to connect to during this time.

With all the fear that circulates from natural disasters, political instability and unfathomable violence, the peacock reminds us to be present to what is true about us. We are magnificent spiritual beings who are forever in the presence of Spirit who guides and protects us. Awakening to this truth at this time is the perfect antidote to any fear we may feel.

As I turn away from conditions and circumstances, I see the benevolent nature of Spirit that dwells within me and guides me on my path. My soul is safe and secure for I am always in God's loving care.

_____

_____

_____

_____

Fear to *faith*

The power of the human mind to stop us from following our divine urge is incredibly strong. I know many people right now who have clearly heard Spirit's calling to go bigger in their lives, but they are stuck in fear: "What if I fail?" "I don't know if I can really do this." "Who am I to do that?" These questions and statements paralyze them, preventing them from following what is obviously theirs to do.

The mind is simply creating a barrier to avoid change — and it can't help itself. It doesn't like it when we transform our identity, and that is what happens when we move forward and grow. Spirit is all about pulling us out of our comfort zone so we can be who we were born to be. Are we going to allow our minds to keep us small, or are we going to follow Spirit's calling and soar into the life that is truly ours to live?

I am ready to follow Spirit *as It gives me the confidence to embrace a greater life for myself. I am no longer influenced by limiting thoughts, for my attention is completely focused on Spirit's guiding light.*

154

Our consciousness is an amazing place with so many different levels of existence. We always have the ability to move from one level to the next, just like an elevator takes us to different floors of a building. Sometimes it may seem as though we are stuck on a lower level and have no power to move ourselves up, but we do. Using tools like affirmations, prayer, inspirational reading, listening to music or taking a walk will move us up.

This morning I didn't even realize I was hanging out on a lower level of my consciousness until I started listening to music. As the beautiful melodies began to play, I could feel my mind relax and let go of all that I had been focused on, freeing me to rise up to the penthouse floor of my consciousness.

Today I exercise my ability to raise *my consciousness to a higher level by doing something that speaks to my soul.*

Identity is a tricky thing. I have found that the more I walk this Earth, the less restricted I am with who I think I am. None of us is locked into an identity. We are not who our parents led us to believe we are; we are not our experiences. We are all expressions of Spirit, and we can change our identity at any moment.

This morning my inner voice asked me who I wanted to be today, and I realized it isn't about being something concrete; it is about being a quality of Spirit, and there are so many to choose from. I asked myself: Do I want to be love, peace, joy, beauty, grace or something else? How cool is it to choose to be a quality of God and just let the day unfold from that choice.

Today, I answer the question "Who am I?" by stating the qualities of Spirit that I am. My day unfolds beautifully when I recognize the spiritual essence of my being.

Fear to *faith*

Today I pulled a thorn out of my psyche that has been restricting my power. I have been feeling its presence for a while, but today is the day I had the courage to look at it and identify it so I could remove it. This got me thinking about the story of Androcles and the lion. Androcles was a slave who, after escaping his master, met a lion in the wilderness. The lion had a thorn it its paw which Androcles removed, and the lion loved him forever.

This is the perfect analogy for how we liberate ourselves from our mental pain. When we are ready to truly be free, we have to go into the wilderness of our minds so we can remove the thorns that crimp our power and strength. This allows us to move forward in life without any inner restrictions.

I am ready to live in freedom, *so I remove all the mental thorns that disable me, and my power and strength are restored.*

_____

_____

_____

_____

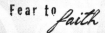

The word "compensate" is on my mind today, especially as it pertains to making up for that which we did not receive in our childhoods. I spent many years of my life attempting to compensate for the unconditional love that was absent during my childhood, and I made some really poor choices along the way. It wasn't until I started deepening my spirituality that the need to compensate was stilled.

I realized that returning to a state of wholeness and unconditional love was not about making up for that which I did not receive as a child. It was about reconnecting with the lost part of myself where love is freely given and peace is a constant. It was about finding the soul of me and the divinity that lies within me.

I am balanced and peaceful knowing that I carry all the love of the universe within my heart.

158

Language is one of the greatest tools human beings have developed for communication. I can't even imagine a world without language, especially because I love to write. However, language does have its limits. Even though it provides us with a common ground of understanding that allows us to relate and convey information, there is still so much room for misunderstanding due to our individual cognitive and perceptual differences.

There is another language we use that is beyond words, one that comes from our energy and our emotions. I know my empathic friends know exactly what I am talking about. Using this non-linear method of communication is powerful because energy and feelings don't lie like words can.

As much as I love language, I know that communicating through my feelings and energy are the most honest methods of communication because they are connected to the heart rather than the brain.

As I sharpen my ability to understand *what others are saying behind all words, I am able to deepen my connection with all beings. Spirit's language is love, and I aspire to converse from that sacred place.*

There used to be a time in my life when I would cringe if someone would say they were slowing down. I used to think that meant disconnecting from life and deteriorating. Now I see it as incredibly positive.

Slowing down now means to me the act of stepping out of the frenzied current of doing and going so that the presence of Spirit is visible. Slowing down allows us to see the God winks, the beauty and synchronicity that is always before us.

I am delighted to slow down knowing this allows me to see Spirit expressing Itself in the most wonderful ways.

160

In our eternal quest to improve ourselves and deepen our spirituality, we must acknowledge how far we have come on this journey. One of my favorite parts of the work I do is witnessing the dramatic transformations my clients experience. Most of them are totally different people within a year.

There is no greater joy for me than watching people liberate themselves from the prison of old beliefs that stifled their self-expression and ability to live the life of their dreams.

Today I encourage you to recognize and celebrate the growth you have made in your life and honor the wonderful unique expression of Spirit that you are.

Today I recognize the immense growth I have made on my journey in this life, and I love and appreciate who I am. I see myself as an ever-evolving spiritual being forever spiraling upward, and I am grateful Spirit guides me every step of the way.

The more I learn about grief, the more I see the impact it has on our lives when it is not fully processed. Until I began my spiritual journey, I saw grief as something to ignore, something time would heal. I believed that I must keep my focus forward and march on.

Although grief is a painful process, today I look at it as a necessary ritual that honors how deeply I loved and appreciated something or someone in my life. When we love someone or something so deeply, we are inextricably bound to it. When it is no longer physically present in our lives, we hurt, and we need to allow ourselves to do whatever we need to do (as long as it isn't destructive) and feel whatever we need to feel in order to recover.

It is ok to fall apart when loss occurs; it is ok to not feel quite right. That is part of grief, and we must honor our individual path through it.

As I experience grief, I don't rush myself through it or force myself to feel better. I honor every step of my journey as I recover from loss, knowing Spirit's loving presence is guiding me every step of the way.

Recently I have been living on the so-called "skinny branch." I have put myself out in the spiritual community in ways I have never done before, stepping massively outside of my comfort zone. There are no maps and no directions — just me and Spirit co-creating a whole lot of new stuff.

In self-development, doing things outside of our comfort zone is always encouraged. However, I think clarification is needed. I don't think we need to bungee jump, sky dive or do anything that puts us in physical danger. I think the barrier that needs to be dissolved involves listening to and acting on the yearnings of the heart rather than surrendering to insecurities that cause us to resist those yearnings. Many of us have been trained to doubt the soul stirrings that expand us. Now is the time to embrace them and fly.

I embrace my soul's yearnings with passion and enthusiasm, as I say "yes" to the path that is rising up for me to walk on. Feelings of insecurity no longer have power over me. God is my Source and is making it easy for me to act upon my heart's desires.

With all the planning we do to create the path we would like our life to take, we never have complete control over the unfolding or the outcome of those plans. One of my favorite sayings is, "When I make plans, God laughs." The uncertainty of life can cause us great anxiety and fear as the mind will oftentimes entertain possibilities of failure, loss and distress as to what awaits us.

This fear can be neutralized by remembering the presence of God in our lives. If I know that Spirit is all good and always demonstrates Its goodness in my life, then it really doesn't matter if my plans don't go the way I intended. Even though allowing Spirit to adjust our life course can be unnerving, knowing that It is working behind the scenes of our lives should bring us great peace. After all, God knows better than we do.

I no longer feel fear when my plans change, for I know that God has a better idea for the manifestation of my good.

Fear to *faith*

164

Fairy tales are so rich in spiritual lessons. For example, Cinderella is the story about transformation, as she shifts from a consciousness of lack, limitation and separation from Spirit to realizing her spiritual magnificence and the unlimited abundance that is hers to have.

Deep within all of us is the knowing of our spiritual nobility, but our life experiences may have caused us to lose sight of that truth. It is a sacred moment when we open the treasure chest of our mind, and we pull out the truth that has been hidden from view. The truth is that we are not impoverished beings; we are rich beyond measure because God is our Source, and we are worthy and deserving of having a fulfilling and rich life fit for a king or queen.

I see the divine majesty of my soul, knowing I am the recipient of Spirit's goodness in all forms. I live in God's excellence, and experience a life that is full and abundant.

Fear to *faith*

There has been so much written about the dark night of the soul. I have experienced that journey many times throughout my life, as many of you have as well. However, I have recently been rethinking the concept. When we have experiences that thrust us into darkness, separation, desolation and fear, I don't think it is the soul that is experiencing the darkness — I think it is our minds.

I believe that our souls are pure light, and the wisdom of Spirit that is nestled deep within us knows nothing of darkness. To heal from the dark night of the soul, it is not the soul that needs to transform; it is our consciousness.

This brings me great peace because knowing that it is not my soul that is experiencing darkness but is rather an experience of my mind, my healing is just a thought away.

My soul is always in a state of harmony and peace for it is made of the pure light of Spirit. Anything that disrupts that peace is caused by my reaction to life, so after I allow the human in me to be fully expressed, Spirit returns me to love.

166

The funny thing about Earth School is that you never know when your exams are going to take place. They just come out of nowhere, so you cannot study, prepare or cram the night before. Unbeknownst to me, last week was finals week for me. Two recurring life lesson themes appeared within a few days of each other. I did my best to navigate through the experiences with greater awareness, which required me to dive deeply into my psyche and my spirituality.

As intense and challenging as these tests can be, they afford us the possibility of the most profound transformations, the outcome of which is our inner freedom.

As life lessons appear, I mindfully walk through these experiences so that all is healed with love and wisdom. Spirit always provides me with the perfect opportunities to work through the unfinished business of my life.

Fear to *faith*

In Greek mythology, there is a river in the underworld called Lethe, which is the river of forgetfulness. It is said that in order to reincarnate, souls must drink from Lethe and forget their past lives so they can live anew. I have often wondered if a certain amount of forgetting is necessary to move forward and create a new life for ourselves. It is a law of nature that we must release in order to receive. Even the word "forget" implies receiving — "for" meaning purpose and "get" meaning receiving.

The idea of forgetting our past may evoke feelings of resistance, as our past defines us. We may say it is impossible to forget our past because our minds are wired to remember for a reason. However, I think this idea has merit and is worth considering no matter how impossible it may seem. If we want to bring in the new, we have to release the old.

Forgetting the past frees me to live in the present and create a boundless future that reflects my highest potential. I soar with Spirit as I move forward in life with energy and love.

168

Given the world we live in, our programming and the nature of the mind, it is vitally important for us to survey our consciousness every day and see if we are experiencing constriction, lack or limitation in any area of our life. Our natural state of being is freedom, and if we aren't feeling free, then we have work to do.

Like everything in life, freedom is a state of mind that we create and maintain. Deepening our spirituality is one way to cultivate inner freedom. When we live in the awareness that we are more than this human existence, we activate the freedom of our soul, and we expand. We become empowered and peaceful, and we are able to see beyond what this world has taught us.

Today I liberate myself from any beliefs that prevent me from living in freedom. Knowing that God is my Source strengthens my faith and fills me with peace as I see the endless good that is forever demonstrating in my life.

This morning I was blessed to see the sunrise in the mountains. Watching the colors on the horizon transform from dark purple to soft orange to yellow as the light grew brighter with the rising of the sun, I recognized the lesson nature was teaching me at that moment. I realized that I have been overlooking the beauty that is present throughout the transitions that connect each stage and cycle of my life. I have been focusing on the discomfort that arises when I am changing rather than the natural beauty that is unfolding before me and through me.

The harmony of Spirit is forever revealing Itself in each moment of life, no matter what we are experiencing, providing us with a higher understanding of life through the rhythm and beauty of this naturally perfect world Spirit created for us to enjoy.

Today I choose to see the transitions of my life through new eyes, and the beauty is clear to me. All life unfolds through the divine pattern of Universal Intelligence, and I can now appreciate the blessings of change.

Fear to *faith*

170

There are so many places to explore within ourselves that facilitate our healing. Once we find those places, it isn't always easy to just march right in and start looking around. Yesterday, when I was doing some inner work, I bumped into one of those places. The feeling I was experiencing drew me to the threshold of where I needed to go, but there was a rusty gate in front of it. I felt paralyzed and powerless as I stared at the rust and realized the gate had not been opened for a long time. I knew I wasn't ready to figure out how to dissolve the corrosion so I could enter.

This reminds me that on the path of self-healing, there are times when we aren't quite ready or equipped to cross into certain places within ourselves until more work is done and we have the tools to meet whatever awaits us to heal. However, just seeing the rusty gate activates an awareness of where we need to go to heal our wounds. When we are ready, we will know exactly where to go, and the gate will open with ease.

I honor my healing journey knowing that it unfolds organically. There is no rush to uncover everything that needs to be seen at once. Each discovery is revealed when I am ready to see it.

Fear to *faith*

It is said that we are all instruments of the Divine and when we are tuned into the harmony of the universe, life flows smoothly, and we experience peace. Just like instruments, we need to take time to spiritually tune ourselves every day. If any part of ourselves is not at the right pitch, the music that is our life is discordant and unnerving. We all have a spiritual tuning fork in the form of prayer, nature or meditation that we can use to bring us into perfect pitch with our Divine nature.

Today I tune myself to Spirit, *and the music of my life is pure delight. I am mindful of anything that causes me to go out of tune, and I use my spiritual tuning fork to bring me back in alignment with Source.*

172

Crying is such a beautiful and natural expression of emotion. I don't know how our society became so resistant to it, rushing us through it when it happens and discouraging us from publicly displaying our sorrows. Over the past week, I have been in the presence of many tears and have shed my own as well. To catch the tears of another is one of the greatest gifts we can give to someone. To be held in love and compassion so that we can safely express our sadness gives our soul freedom and allows us to heal our hearts.

I see the divine beauty in shedding tears and catching the tears of others. Tears are simply flowing energy that contain the grace of God.

I will forever be in awe at the ease in which a belief can be discharged from our consciousness, permanently changing our entire outlook on life. As I continually create my life, I notice that I attach myself to a belief system and stay there for a while. Then something happens that uproots the belief, and a whole new wonderful world opens up for me that I never considered. That is when I say to myself, "What was I thinking?" Oh, the fun of this life journey! This is why I don't take myself too seriously. The constant turnover of old beliefs keeps my mind in a state of flexibility so that I can expand into a bigger better life with a sense of humor.

I keep my mind open to changing beliefs I have outgrown, knowing that more evolved beliefs take their place that expand my soul.

174

Every significant person or animal who comes into our lives makes an impression upon our hearts. Their souls create an imprint that stays with us forever, even when they are no longer in our lives. Regardless why a loved one leaves our life, the hand-print or paw print they leave on our heart can never be taken away from us. How they changed us, inspired us or just loved us is forever a part of us. Each of these imprints is woven together into the fabric of our heart and creates a tapestry of love that eternally enfolds us.

I am grateful for every hand and paw that has impressed its love upon my heart. I know I am forever connected to those I have shared a loving relationship with for we are bound together in the one life of Spirit.

Our lives exist in between Earth and the sky, and both supply us with everything we need — not just physically but spiritually as well. As I survey my life, I see that there have been parts where I have been grounded on Earth and parts where I have been floating in the sky. Today I see the necessity of living equally in both worlds in order to be spiritually balanced and able to live life to the fullest.

In my mind, the sky symbolizes the spacious freedom of vast possibilities; it is where we discover fresh ideas to bring newness into our lives. Earth symbolizes the manifestation of those ideas in form. If I'm living solely in the sky, then nothing gets created, and I will be stuck in formless space. If I'm living solely in the earth, then my life is stagnant and nothing new is being introduced to take on form.

Living in both worlds allows us to discover new ideas and bring them into form so we can evolve and expand. This is how we were meant to live.

Today I see the value of living in between earth and sky as I use both worlds to create a life of harmony and joy.

Fear to *faith*

176

The process of reclaiming our power and living authentically requires us to change how we view ourselves. As we grow, we are no longer who we thought we were, and we have to adjust to that. At first we may find it unsettling because we don't recognize who we are. Being aware of this step in our expansion allows us to move through our transformation more comfortably because we know what to expect, and we don't resist it. Surrendering to the new "us" opens the door for our evolution to take on greater momentum so we can live in freedom.

I am excited to get to know the new me *as I surrender my old identity and embrace the magnificence of who I truly am.*

_____

_____

_____

_____

_____

_____

_____

_____

_____

Fear to *faith* _____

Tug of war isn't just a children's game; it is a state of consciousness. Challenging decisions, directional changes and relationship conflicts are just a few things that cause us to engage in this game. Many of us unconsciously use the inner tug of war as a problem-solving technique, but oftentimes it just creates more stress. We can only stay in this state of being for so long for it creates paralysis and constriction.

Here's an idea: Let go of the rope. Letting go of the rope may feel uncomfortable, but if the tug of war is a stalemate, then letting go ends the struggle. Letting go breaks the energy so that Spirit can guide us to the perfect solution that allows us to move forward. Tugging only creates restriction. Letting go creates expansion.

Today I drop the rope and walk away from any inner tug of war that is taking place within my consciousness. I am filled with peace as I can now see Spirit's presence guiding me to a greater understanding.

178

Whenever we are learning something new, we follow the instruction we are given in order to fully master the new skill. However, what I have found is that after the instruction is complete, I usually need to diverge a little bit from what I have learned and make it my own. For me, that is the fun part. If we do not combine what we are taught with who we are and create our own unique way of doing things, then the world will never progress. We will just be doing things the same way they have always been done.

Everything I learn opens up the deep well of wisdom within me that allows me to express myself in new ways that bring creative ideas to the world.

_____
_____
_____
_____
_____
_____
_____
_____

Fear to *faith*

Today I realized how many conversations I should have had with people instead of silently walking away from relationships. Sometimes it takes a lot of courage to give voice to feelings that may result in an uncomfortable conversation. Although I have made a lot of progress in this area, I still have work to do. I have come to realize that keeping silent creates unfinished business in my life, and that is no longer acceptable to me.

I courageously engage in conversations that may be uncomfortable as I allow myself to speak my truth no matter the outcome. This allows me to live in freedom and be clear and clean in all my relationships.

Fear to *faith*

I have spent a lot of time contemplating the effect of punishment on our spirituality. As a child, I was punished by the hand and by isolation for my transgressions. As a result, I became my own punisher as I entered adulthood. I used to think there was purpose in maintaining a punishing attitude toward myself; I attributed my ability to be successful and my drive for excellence to self-punishment. The inner threat motivated me to do well ... or else!

I am so grateful that I now see the error of my thinking. I no longer need to use self-punishment as a motivational tool to do well in life. Although it worked for a little while, it really hurt my spirit and created a huge divide within my beingness. I have come to believe that if we love ourselves unconditionally and treat ourselves with kindness and compassion, we will naturally be motivated to excel in our lives. By being kind and loving toward myself, I naturally do well in anything I choose to do in my life.

Spirit is the great motivating force in my life, and as I treat myself with respect, the floodgates are flung wide open for my good to come pouring into my life.

Fear to *faith*

This morning my mind took me to a place of fear because I thought something I love was in jeopardy of being removed from my life. Not wanting to stay in a place of helplessness and anxiety, I had to dig deep and remember that underneath all loss are new opportunities pushing their way to the surface. The gap between loss and new growth can be scary because we cannot see the newness with our eyes, so we must lean into our faith and trust that Spirit keeps everything moving forward in our lives and would never leave us hanging in an abyss.

Knowing that loss is a temporary state of being, I trust that Spirit always brings new opportunities into my life that are meaningful and fulfilling.

182

As we walk along our life path and create our journey, we often ask ourselves, "What do I want my life to look like? What do I want to experience?" Those are wonderful questions, but do we ever ask the question, "How do I want to feel about myself?" In my mind, that question should come before all others, especially if we have self-doubt or we don't like aspects of ourselves. Our relationship with ourselves is primary; if we don't love ourselves unconditionally and trust ourselves, then regardless of all the stuff we have or things we do, life will never be quite right. Restoring our inner wholeness and self-love is the key to a truly fulfilling and happy life.

I am ready to let go of all thoughts that stand in the way of my loving and trusting myself. I now see myself as a divine expression of Spirit, and I am perfect just as I am.

Fear to *faith*

One of my favorite analogies is seeing our lives as a movie, and we play all the roles that are involved in the production of that movie. This morning I realized I have been in the actor role playing the character I created for myself so I could express that part of me that needed to be expressed. However, it is time for me to shift into the role of screenwriter because there are changes I am ready to make to my life movie. It is really empowering to know that we are the creators of our life journey; we write the script, and we can make changes any time we please.

I am the creator of my life, and I pay attention to inner yearnings that are beckoning me to make changes to my path. The universe always supports my decisions that lead me to greater self-expression and joy.

184

There are so many different tools and strategies for us to use to anchor ourselves in the here and now. God gave us one that is always available to us, and it is free — breathing. When I stop and really think about the breath, I am overwhelmed with awe and gratitude, because I know I take it for granted. Since the day we are born, our lungs have been allowing us to live on this place called Earth and experience this precious life. Whenever my mind hijacks me and I lose my way, I come back to my breath. When I breathe with conscious intent and gratitude, I become present and aware of this gift of life.

As I bring my awareness to my breath, my mind relaxes, and I am able to see the beauty and splendor of the life I am living.

Fear to *faith*

Many people who set foot on the spiritual path want to deepen their spirituality as quickly as possible. They jump right into the deep end and take every class, read every book and do all the spiritual practices they can fit into their day. I am one of those people who did that, and the result of my zealous attempt to be spiritually perfect backfired on me. I became so dependent on "doing" spirituality that I wasn't being it, and I wasn't connecting with my natural spirituality that is not dependent on books or practices.

Even though learning about spirituality and doing our practices is an important part in developing our connection to God, there is another part that is equally important, and that is discovering our own unique connection to Spirit. This is something that cannot be learned; it can only be found, for it has always been with us.

I connect to Spirit in my own way, and I feel vibrant and alive. God is beyond words and human concepts, and I am grateful I can sense Its loving presence at all times.

186

As our world becomes ever more interesting, I find myself needing to be reminded of who my Source is. It is not people, governments or anything that is tangible. It is God. With all the distractions and drama that are happening in our country right now, today I pause, breathe and remember that God is bigger than anything my human eyes can see. This is but a snapshot, and instead of collapsing and contracting into fear, I expand my consciousness, deepen my faith and trust that there is something bigger being revealed. I do my part by opening up the space for divine harmony and love to show up in the most amazing way possible.

I find peace in Spirit's presence within me, as I relax in the knowing that all is unfolding through divine right action and order.

Fear to *faith*

I have always been fascinated by Chinese medicine because it is holistic in nature and views illness as an imbalance, not just in the body but in the spirit and the energy systems as well. Using this approach, if you were to get a cold, you wouldn't say, "I have a cold." Instead, you would say, "I have an imbalance."

One of the greatest causes of imbalance is stress. It disrupts the harmony and flow of our entire beingness. However, our minds are a great tool for us to use to restore our balance. At the onset of stress, our first reaction should be to reinstate harmony through our consciousness. After all, stress is a state of mind, and we have control over our minds. The more we exercise our ability to shift from stress to peace, the greater balance we will have in our body, mind and energy systems, which will lead to greater health.

I disengage my mind from anything that is causing me to feel stress, and I relax into the divine harmony that is the underlying current of my being. All is well.

I never realized how sensitive I was to the word "goodbye" until I took a class on grief recovery. At our last class, we had a closing ritual in which each person said a few words to every student, followed by the word "goodbye." When the instructor first explained the ritual to us, I protested within myself. I didn't want to say goodbye to anyone. We had shared deep and personal stories with each other, and the last thing I wanted to do was let go of these beloved souls.

My lesson was before me. Letting go is a huge part of life, and even though people leave our lives, we are never alone. Not only is Spirit always present, but as we let go, we create space for new people to enter our lives who will touch our souls as much as those who have left.

I know that every goodbye leads to hello, so I courageously open my heart to all relationships knowing each connection enhances my life. Spirit is my constant companion, and It eternally shows up as loving people in my life.

Normally when we think about relationships, we think about individual people we are connected to. However, there is another relationship we all have in common, and that is our relationship with society at large. Everyone has a different concept of what society is and a different attitude toward it. We cannot help but be affected by it because it is part of the human experience. What we can do is become mindful of how it impacts our beliefs about ourselves and if it causes us to question who we are. Sometimes we may compare ourselves to the norms it represents, which can inhibit us from being the unique individual expressions of Spirit that we are.

Let us remember that society is just an idea. It is important for us to ask ourselves if we are using it as a weapon against ourselves to prevent us from being all that we are, as different as that may be, for the sake of playing it safe and conforming to what might be called normal.

Although I appreciate society, I know its purpose is not to hinder my self-expression. I allow myself to be who I am, no matter how different that may be, for that allows me to bring my unique gifts and qualities to this world.

190

We were all born with the ability to ride the different waves of life that come our way. Some are fun and easy, while others are unwieldy and challenging. Each wave has its own energy and motion, so if we focus in on it, we can figure out how to stay on top and ride the wave all the way to the shore without getting pulled under and wiping out. The same holds true for the waves of life. If we keep our minds focused on the nature of what we are experiencing, we can stay on top of it and ride it through to its completion instead of losing our balance and getting dragged underneath and wiping out.

I am a surfer of life, and I ride the waves of my life with grace and ease. I keep my mind clear and focused as Spirit guides me safely to shore.

Throughout my childhood, my mom was very uptight and judgmental. As she aged, she softened up and became more relaxed. When I was in my 30s, we had a conversation where she told me she was no longer bothered by the things that used to bother her. I remember being surprised by that because she had been so anchored in her opinions and behaviors, and at that time in my life, I couldn't understand how a person could just stop being bothered by things. Today, I totally get what she was saying. I now know how flexible the mind really is and how important it is to not allow anything to hijack our energy and emotions and rob us of our peace of mind.

As the curator of my consciousness, I am able to keep my mind calm and peaceful no matter what is going on in my world.

_____

_____

_____

_____

_____

_____

_____

_____

192

Competition and war have been mainstays of humankind forever. For most of my life, I surrendered to the idea that this is just how we are as human beings, and I have to accept it. However, I have come to believe that humankind is capable of better. As our consciousness evolves and our world becomes smaller, I don't think we have to continue indulging in competition and war. It has clearly come to the point where our survival is at stake if these primitive behaviors persist. I think it is totally possible for cooperation to replace war and competition, but I leave the how of it up to Spirit. Since cooperation is based on love and support, everyone wins when our goal is to help one another.

I believe that all beings can thrive by living in cooperation with one another, and I hold that vision so that peace, love and harmony can prevail in our world.

Fear to *faith*

Recently, when I was driving home on the freeway from Los Angeles, my car started veering off to the right, and I realized it had gotten terribly windy. The faster I went, the more difficult it was to control my car, so naturally, I slowed down. It dawned on me that a life analogy had just been revealed to me. When life circumstances cause us to swerve and we experience fear and get hyped up by stress, we lose control. We crash. However, if we slow down and pay attention to what is unfolding, we won't get swept up in the fear, and we can navigate through the circumstance with care and ease.

As I travel through my life, I slow down when the winds of change blow, allowing me to peacefully move through the experience.

194

Many of us in spiritual communities use common words and phrases to describe enlightened and unenlightened states of being. We use phrases such as high vibration, low vibration or high frequency, low frequency. While I was flipping through the television channels yesterday, amused by the superficial nature of some of the programming, I realized that perhaps differing levels of consciousness are not so much about high or low but more about shallow or deep. Intentionally plumbing the depths of consciousness and living in a deep state of awareness has not yet reached critical mass in our culture. Hanging out in the shallow waters of the psyche is far more popular. Going deep is where our healing lies, but it does take courage. Although I totally understand why people choose to live in shallow waters, I also know they are missing out on the hidden power that lies in the depth of their being.

I courageously dive into the deep waters of my soul to find the treasures that reveal who I am. Spirit accompanies me on my inner journey to freedom and gives me the love and strength to transform my life.

Fear to *faith*

In Hollywood, there is a concept referred to as "going off script," which means you unexpectedly stop following the script and do your own thing. Whenever I experience constriction or boredom in my life because I feel as though I am just doing what I am supposed to do based on roles I am playing and expectations I have placed upon myself, I know it is time to go off script and draw my direction from a deeper source — Spirit. Following roles and scripts isn't necessarily a bad thing because it can give us focus and purpose. However, we outgrow the roles and the scripts as our lives evolve, and there inevitably comes a time when we have to create something new.

Going off the script of my life allows me to take my life in a new direction that comes from the spontaneous and creative nature of my soul. I follow God's lead, and my spirit is rejuvenated as I create my life anew.

196

I believe that when we came into this world, before our experiences altered us and our ego became the dominator of our consciousness, we innately knew of our oneness with God. There was no belief in separation, and we lived in a state of pure, unconditional love. It is my belief that all healing lies in reconnecting to this state of being. If we can reach back beyond the experiences that have led us to feel guilty, ashamed, unworthy, and/or self-loathing and remember who we were when we arrived here and identify with the pure Divine energy of our soul instead of our ego, all will be healed.

As I reconnect with the purity of my soul, I am awash in the unconditional love of Spirit that returns me to my innate understanding of the expression of Spirit that I am.

Fear to *faith*

The idea of perfection has always intrigued me. As a child, I strove for it; as an adult, I question it. Perfection as it is known in our culture is all about achieving some sort of ideal that reflects a flawless state of being. This definition of perfection is relative and fleeting.

However, there is another type of perfection that is eternal and meaningful, and that is the perfection of God. Our universe is absolutely perfect for it is governed by love and law, and the action of life is simply cause and effect. So anything that is happening in our lives is absolutely perfect because it is following universal law. When we awaken to seeing perfection in this way, we can let go of needing to meet ideals and recognize that we are perfect beings created by a perfect God.

As I see myself as the expression of God's perfection, I let go of the need to be flawless in the eyes of society.

198

I have noticed that sometimes those of us who study spirituality fall into the belief that in order to be truly free and happy, we must become egoless and eradicate all thought. While I understand the concept, I think that if we are egoless and without thought, we are no longer in human form. The purpose of mindful, spiritual living is not about eliminating mental processes but understanding them and learning how to use them positively. The ego and thoughts have purpose; they allow us to get along in this world, make decisions and survive. The key is for us to be the master of them, not to get rid of them.

I appreciate the way my mind works and my ability to understand it and use it wisely and constructively. Spirit gave me a mind to evolve my soul, and I am grateful for how it serves me.

Fear to *faith*

Catching ourselves in our thought patterns is no simple task. There isn't an alarm we can set to interrupt us when we are going down a road of thought that is placing us in limitation. What we can do is set the intention to be aware and mindful and meditative. These two practices — mindfulness and meditation — will create a gap that allows us to take notice when we are caught in a constricting thought stream. Our minds are wired to conserve energy, so we create thinking shortcuts. Oftentimes these shortcuts prevent us from being present to other possibilities of experience because we make assumptions based on past results. We can improve the quality of our lives simply by catching ourselves when we say, "This is going to happen because that is how it always turns out," and changing our thought to, "I am open to seeing a wonderful outcome this time."

I am creating a consciousness that allows me to be aware of when I am preventing myself from experiencing a rich and abundant life.

200

I have been thinking recently about my life before I plunged into developing my spirituality. One of the biggest changes I made to my consciousness is really knowing and believing that I am one with all life and God, and I am never alone. However, I will never forget what it felt like to experience alienation and separation on a daily basis. I now know that I felt that way because I had a subconscious belief that I was alone in this world, I was separated from God, and I was different from everyone. Clearly my inner world was being mirrored in my experience of life. Once I realized the truth of who I am and changed that belief, I never felt separate or alone again.

As I recognize my eternal oneness with all life, I realize I am never alone. Knowing I am connected to all beings through the one heart of Spirit brings me great joy.

When most people think about using prayer, they or someone they know are in some sort of crisis. However, prayer is something we can use for any shift we would like to experience in our lives, no matter what it is. I know many people who would like to feel differently within themselves; they want to deepen their faith, have more confidence or be more engaged with life. These are all great opportunities for prayer.

Prayer creates the path for change to happen, so we should be using it whenever we are ready to improve any area of our lives. Spirit gave us the gift of prayer to be able to use Its power, and it works.

I broaden my understanding of prayer and use it whenever I desire any sort of change within me or my life. I know that the universe always acts on my prayers and brings them to life.

202

Oneness is a big concept in spirituality. Recognizing our oneness with all life dissolves the barriers created by that which separates us through religion, socioeconomics, culture, etc. But there is another type of oneness that isn't always discussed: oneness with the self. So many of us have divisions within our own psyche that keep us at odds with ourselves. Anytime we condemn ourselves for a mistake we have made, or a miscalculation or criticize parts of ourselves, we diminish our wholeness.

To live in oneness with the self, we need to see ourselves as God sees us and love all parts of ourselves unconditionally. As soon as we do, we will experience oneness within, which makes it much easier to experience oneness with all life.

I experience oneness within my soul as I love and accept all parts of who I am. As I see myself through the eyes of Spirit, I see others in the same light, knowing we are one.

The importance of creative self-expression can never be underestimated. It is the driving force of our life journey. Oftentimes we turn our backs on that part of us that is totally creative. Since we are continually outgrowing our lives, we must be able to create new patterns and things for us to do and be, and we can't do that if we are closed off to the creative impulse that is our unlimited source for new ideas. Creativity is Spirit in action, and it is there for all of us to use and use often.

The creative power of Spirit gives *me the ability to evolve and expand myself in wonderful and amazing ways.*

204

One of the most challenging life lessons for me has been cultivating the ability to stand in truth while watching someone go through debilitating physical changes. I used to get really upset that this happens to people, but as I turned to Spirit for guidance, I realized I must elevate my consciousness and see things through the eyes of God.

Each one us has our own path that we co-create with Spirit, so when we see beyond the human and recognize that all of life is governed by Spirit no matter what it looks like to our minds, we can find acceptance and peace. When we stand in truth, everything looks different. There is no fear, only understanding and peace. When we can see beyond the human shell that we occupy and celebrate the eternal nature of our soul that cannot be harmed and has infinite possibilities of experiences to choose from, all is well.

As I stand in truth, I am comfortable with all the cycles of life and experiences that move the spirit forward in its evolution.

Fear to *faith*

Many of us have been taught that we can only have so much good in our lives. As I reach greater heights in my personal success, I find that I need to do mental work so that those old thoughts do not block my expansion. I realize that my mind needs to be loosened up and stretched so I can both receive more and be more. As I stand in my increasing expansion, I say to myself, "I can handle even greater success," and the old limits fall away. We can apply this to all areas of our lives so we can experience greater health, greater financial prosperity, greater creativity and greater love.

There is no lack or limitation in the universe, so I open myself up to receive more than ever, and I am comfortable in the growth this affords me.

206

I must confess I have mixed feelings about the saying "nothing lasts forever." When things are unpleasant, that sentiment brings me joy. When something or someone I love is leaving my life, it brings me sadness. Before I developed my spirituality, the experience of loss was devastating to me because I did not have an interior sense of abundance. When loss hit my life, it only amplified my inner emptiness, making the grieving process that much more difficult.

Today, I experience loss much differently. I know that even though I will miss that person or thing, I still feel whole and abundant inside of myself because Spirit is always with me.

As I connect with the Divine within, I know that I am always rich and abundant in spirit no matter what is entering or exiting my life.

I have always been intrigued by the idea of the shadow. It is such a powerful force when left unexposed for it drives people to destruction, whether that destruction is directed inward or outward. The shadow is just a creation of our fears, and the irony is that because we refuse to look at our fears and keep them in the dark, they become even more frightening.

There is a lot of shadow being expressed in our world right now, but we need to be careful not to allow other people's shadows to become our own. The fear has to stop with us, and one way we can do that is to deepen our spirituality and connection to our Higher Power.

When we stand in the light of truth, fear dissolves. When we no longer allow shadow-driven behavior to rock our world and trust in the power of good to reign supreme, then we have defeated fear.

I illuminate my consciousness with the light of Spirit, and all shadows of fear disappear. I rise up in the awareness that the world is under the direction of divine right order, and I am at peace.

208

When I was in college and trying to figure out a career, I was frustrated because nothing called to me. Of all the possibilities that were presented to me, nothing was a perfect fit. What I was looking for did not exist in my world at that time.

Today I find myself in a similar situation, but it does not relate to my vocation. There is something I would like to see in this world that does not exist, but instead of just accepting that, I am going to bring it into the world. I believe that Spirit is calling all of us to bring something into this world that is not here, whether it is a school, a form of healing or simply more love. As creative, spiritual beings, we have been endowed with the ability to create anything that we are moved to create. The call of Spirit to improve our world is within all of us. The choice to listen is ours.

I am open to being a creative channel for Spirit to work through me to bring what I see is needed in this world. God gives me the strength and direction to do what I know is mine to do.

Today I woke up with the startling awareness that I am at the beginning of recreating my life, and I am overwhelmed as to where to begin. I have projects I could dig into, closets I could clean out, but I am hesitant because I feel I need a period of time to just rest in my soul. I find myself oscillating between thinking I need to do something to move myself forward and just sitting still so I can process what I am experiencing.

When I looked up the Old English origins of the word "begin" I was amazed when I saw that it said "be open." The lesson I get from this is to be open to whatever feels right to do. The beginning is a tender space to be in, and I know that the heart and mind need to work together to forge the best path to create the most fulfilling life for us to live.

As I begin a new life filled with unlimited possibilities, I relax in the knowing that I can take my time and allow my new path to unfold through Spirit's gentle guidance.

Yesterday as I was impatiently sitting through movie trailers in anticipation of a movie I was excited to see, profundity happened. I did not expect words of truth to come blasting through the surround sound — words that landed so deeply in my soul that I was profoundly moved.

Those words were, "Life cannot be restrained; it must break free." These words remind me of the spiritual truth of everyone and everything. Deep within all of us is the divine life urge that yearns to be expressed through us. Although we can try our best to restrain it, there are dire consequences if we do. When we don't allow that life to come out, we suffer and get sick or feel miserable because we are stifling our divine nature.

Everyone expresses this life differently, and it serves our world for all of us to express that life as it appears uniquely through us. The time has come for us to let that life break free.

I recognize the Infinite Life Force that dwells within me, and I give It free reign to express Itself through me by means of me. I trust It and know that living in this state of freedom brings me great joy, health and happiness.

_____

_____

_____

Fear to *faith*

One of the greatest yet most challenging spiritual lessons is finding fulfillment in Spirit rather than in material things. Facing this challenge pushes us to develop a deeper awareness of the invisible presence of God within ourselves and to be able to see how It shows up in our physical lives.

For me, this sacred journey begins in the silence of my soul as I stand in a place of sweet surrender to the One who knows all and is all — God. As I stop asking God to bring me things outside of myself to fill me up, I open up to Its energy, wisdom, love and grace to be my fulfillment. Then I receive the gifts of the universe that are beyond human understanding.

The Divine within me nurtures my soul and provides me with the invisible sustenance that fills me up and restores my wholeness.

212

We cannot overstate the truth: Our energy creates our future. If we feel optimistic, we invite good into our lives. If we worry, we block our good. I have found that when something arises in my life, and I am either looking for solutions or I want to know the outcome, rather than go into worry or stress about having to figure things out, I say to myself with joyful expectation, "I can't wait to see how Spirit is going to work this out."

When I consciously move my energy from concern to excitement, the end result is always good. We have the ability to break the worry habit; it just takes practice by affirming that Spirit always works things out for us when we let It — and taking notice when It does.

I keep my mind in a state of joyful expectation knowing that my life unfolds with ease when I allow Spirit to guide my way.

Fear to *faith*

Being a native Southern Californian, I am quite accustomed to earthquakes. So when the ground shook this morning, I immediately moved into what I call "earthquake consciousness." I do not panic; instead, I become one with the earthquake, carefully gauging if I need to do anything, and I just ride it out.

This consciousness can be applied to any circumstance or situation that shakes us up in our lives. Staying calm and present to what is before us rather than reacting with fear allows us to have the presence of mind to make any decisions that need to be made while we ride out the experience, knowing that eventually the shaking will stop.

Although things may shift around me, the unshakable presence of Spirit within keeps me grounded and centered. I relax in the awareness that I am always safe in God.

214

During a recent conversation with a close friend of mine, I told her that I really wanted to have confirmation for an intuitive feeling I was experiencing about someone in my life. Her response to me was, "You don't need to know." As right as she was, my mind was not happy. It wanted validation for what my spirit was picking up on.

The mind loves to see evidence for what we are perceiving on the subtle energetic wavelengths, but do we really need to appease the mind? Not if we totally trust our intuition. If we stay in the present moment and are patient with the natural unfolding of life, the mind is stilled. Everything gets revealed in due time anyway.

I trust that my heart knows what is true and real even if my mind is skeptical. Spirt reveals the truth through my heart, and that is all I need to know.

As human beings, we cannot help setting expectations as to how we would like our lives to unfold. This is completely natural. However, something else that is natural is what might be called interference with our plans. I know in my heart that we are all under the direction of a Higher Intelligence that coordinates the movement of the planets and our little lives, so I trust that anything that "interferes" with my expectations is a good thing. I may have a moment of disappointment when this happens, but I am quick to remind myself that there is a better way for my good to unfold, so I take a step back and watch the magic of the universe do its thing.

I hold lightly to my plans for I know that God is the great director of how my good is to unfold in my life. Therefore, I recognize that any interference in those plans is Spirit opening up a better way for my good to be made manifest.

Hunger and craving are not confined to the physical realm of our existence. Our spirit hungers and craves freedom and self-expression, and when we starve it from what it needs, we look for other ways to satisfy it by eating too much food, indulging in excessive sex, over-spending or gambling, just to name a few distractions. When we are not conscious of our deepest spiritual needs and make choices of the flesh to satiate our soul, we fall into behaviors that can spiral out of control due to the destruction that can result from the poor choices we are making.

Rather than condemn ourselves for not choosing the right nourishment for our spirit, we must love and forgive ourselves and ask our spirit what it really needs to feel nourished and fulfilled. And then we must give it what it needs. Sometimes that can mean making difficult decisions that impact our relationships and result in major life changes. But a malnourished soul must be fed what it needs so we live happy, healthy, joy-filled lives.

Today I listen to the yearnings of my soul and give it what it needs so that it is well fed. With God's loving strength and support, I know I can make any changes to my life that honor my spirit's deepest desires.

When I was a young child, my mom told me that we do not get everything we desire in life. That belief stayed with me until I began studying Science of Mind. Thank God I learned that you can have it all. This wonderful truth made me aware of all the compromising I had done throughout the course of my life. I truly believed I had to just settle for what came into my life even though my spirit was not fulfilled. It is so easy to look backwards and see the errors of my thinking in the choices I made in the past.

I still struggle when that awareness hits me between the eyes in my present life, and I realize I have fallen back into the old habit of compromising. When my spirit rises up and tells me I need to rethink a decision, I cannot deny it. Then my faith is seriously put to the test because I have to trust that there is a better choice to make that does not require me to compromise a thing.

I know that all of my soul's desires are showing up in my life in the perfect way and time through Spirit's divine direction.

Fear to *faith*

218

We spend a lot of time involved in conversation — whether we are in a conversation, witnessing a conversation or having a conversation with ourselves. This is how we express our thoughts and ideas and connect with each other, so it makes sense that this activity is a constant for us. It behooves us to pay attention to the energy we are investing in all conversations we are participating in because that energy impacts our life force. We can create deep inner peace by being mindful about how conversations are affecting us. Are we getting polluted by the conversations we are in or exposing ourselves to? If so, it is time for us to clear the air.

Today I pay attention to all conversations that are in my sphere of influence, and I become the gatekeeper of all that enters my consciousness. I only permit that which is life affirming to take up residence in my mind, and I reject anything that is harmful to me. I am the master of my inner universe, and I have all the power to keep myself in a peaceful state.

Fear to *faith*

The practice of centering ourselves in Spirit is helpful in staying grounded as we go through our various life experiences. When we invest our energy in fear, we are pulled off center, and we fall apart. It is vitally important for us to move our awareness back to the divine center of our being when this happens so we can live in peace. When I need to center myself, I close my eyes, put my hands on my heart, and say to myself as many times as needed, "I am home in my soul in the presence of the Divine, grounded and centered in love."

As I center myself in Spirit's boundless love, all fear disappears. This is my natural state of being, and I experience deep joy when I live from this place.

220

We often hear that where there is love, there is no fear. Before I began my spiritual journey, I spent more time in fear because I could only feel deep love if I was in a romantic relationship. Deepening my spirituality totally broke that open. Now I can feel profound love regardless of my relationship status.

When we lean into the love that is beyond the personal, we don't need an object or person to evoke the feeling of love for it is the life force that is always present within us. We just need to call it forth into expression.

Today I see love within and around me, for I know it is the universal energy that connects all life. I invite love to fill me up and put me in right relationship with myself and all beings.

Do you ever stop to think how enslaved you might be by your thoughts, conditions or the opinions of others? Sometimes it is hard to figure out if we are. When I feel like I am being pulled by a strong inner urge or desire that is interrupted by a voice within me that says "no," it is a sign that maybe a thought or belief is holding me back from what my heart desires.

Any thoughts that censure our innate desires are not the truth of who we are, and only we can stop believing they are. We were not meant to live in bondage of any kind. When we allow ourselves to be free of all restraints, we are living in concert with our true self.

Today I claim my inner freedom, and I allow myself to be led by the creative Spirit that dwells within me. I enjoy the spontaneity of life and the peace I experience when I surrender to the divine flow of the universe. Life was meant to be free and creative, and I honor my spirit when I live from this place.

_____

_____

_____

_____

_____

_____

222

Fear and paralysis go hand in hand. When I am afraid, I am stuck. I am not able to flow with the creative energy of my being because the fear is holding me hostage in a frozen state of being. The remedy is clearly action and movement, which has many forms. Action can mean doing something physical that makes me feel better, or it can be simply changing my consciousness to see things differently.

Today I take the necessary action that moves me to a place of love and peace, and everything in my world changes for the better.

Fear to faith

Many people in the world have an intense need to persuade others to see things their way. If I feel fear when someone is attempting to persuade me to see something a certain way and it does not feel right to me, I remind myself that there is a Power greater than them and their views. That Power is God. Sometimes fear serves as a warning sign that we need to disengage from something that is not right us and to trust ourselves in what we are feeling. I know that any viewpoint that is not life affirming eventually falls apart and turns to dust.

I am not affected *by anyone's attempt to persuade me to see things their way, especially when it does not feel right to me. I stand confidently and strongly in what I see is true and real. I have complete faith that God is governing everything in our world so that eventually all that is not based on love is rendered powerless.*

224

Do you ever feel like your life is crowding in on you and there are a billion things on your mind competing for your attention? With all that we may have going on in our lives and the thinking and problem solving we are engaged in, that inner space can get quite congested, even to the point where we think we might implode. When this happens to me, I know I need to get some perspective and expand my consciousness, so I look at a picture of the Earth from space. This reminds me that I am part of a bigger universe, and what I am experiencing in my little mind is just a speck compared to the vastness of life.

Today I expand my consciousness and see beyond the boundaries of my human mind. It brings me great joy to liberate myself from the confines of my small world, as I explore a spiritual reality that is bigger than anything I have ever known.

Fear to *faith*

When I arrived home after an extra-ordinarily busy day, my first inclination was to plug into my electronic devices and catch up on emails, phone calls and the world. The more I thought about doing that, the more uncomfortable I became. I just wanted to experience peace, so I hit the pause button and relaxed.

I absolutely love the power of the pause, because it allows me to turn away from the demands of the outside world and get centered in my soul. It is refreshing to just be still without having to plug into anything except the Spirit within.

I listen to my soul and press the pause button when I feel the outside world is pulling me apart. I turn within where Spirit lives, and I take refuge there when I need replenishment.

226

There is so much healing that comes from slowing down and getting lost in the beauty that surrounds us. "Stop and smell the roses" is sage advice for us, especially when our world gets hectic and overwhelming. I know that when my life is ramped up and my mind is going a million miles a minute, I am not present to anything.

At any moment of any day, there is something subtle to see or experience that reminds us that it is the simple grace of life that is most important and life giving, not the frenetic energy that distracts us from the beauty of this world.

Today I slow down and really see the beauty that surrounds me, and my spirit is instantly healed. I remind myself of the importance of standing still, breathing and taking in the variety of forms that reflect the divine harmony that is everywhere present. I am grateful for this day and my ability to see the good.

_____

_____

_____

_____

_____

_____

_____

It is said that there is more to our reality than meets the human eye. I find this thought especially comforting when I feel concern about the world. As external events become increasingly unsettling, I know I need to remember that there is so much hidden from my view, and I must move my consciousness from fear to faith. Spirit is the guiding principle underneath all form and situations, and when I anchor myself in that truth, I can be calm, no matter what is going on.

Today I remind myself that God is more powerful than any person or situation, and It is the great balancing energy of the universe. Knowing that Spirit creates harmony and order out of chaos, I have complete faith that this harmony and order are now emerging before my very eyes.

228

Life was not meant to be a struggle. When we turn off our little minds and surrender to Spirit's love and wisdom, the struggle disappears. Easier said than done. We identify so strongly with the contents of our little minds — our culture, our personal history and the mundane thoughts that keep us stuck in one place — that turning it off may seem impossible. If we can just let go for a moment of all that and raise our thought to a higher place where we can connect with the Mind of God, then we can let go of seeing life as a struggle. Although God is invisible, we all have the ability to sense Its presence when we tune in and listen to It.

Today I still my mind and listen to God. There is a higher wisdom within me that understands the language of God, and so I trust that and allow God to guide me. I feel confident in the direction I am being led, for God knows far better than I.

_____

_____

_____

_____

_____

_____

_____

Fear to *faith*

This week I felt like I was deeply en- trenched in the human side of life. Today I realized that I needed to change my focus and move my mind to a higher level and relax in the light of Spirit. I don't need to invest my energy in the affairs of the world today. This is my day to com- mune with God and be restored to a state of peace. Even though I believe it is important for all of us to know what is going on in our world, taking a day off from the in- formation highway is a healthy and restorative practice that brings us back to peace.

I lift my consciousness to a higher plane of thinking, feeling and being as I take in the energy of God and free myself of all discord. I am able to see above the drama of the world and behold the divine order that runs everything in the universe. I release all worries and concerns to God and bask in the beauty of this day.

Fear to *faith*

230

I think it is fair to say that most of us carry around burdens in the form of thoughts, memories and emotions that weigh us down, but we refuse to let them go. Sometimes we feel it is impossible to release them, but the truth is, we absolutely have the power to do so at any time. We don't have to go through a lengthy process to free ourselves from any burden — all we have to do is decide that we are done carrying it, and let it go. The power of decision is strong, especially when we know we have had enough.

Today I make the decision to let go of all burdens, and I delight in the freedom that is now mine to enjoy. God did not create me to live in heaviness, so I gladly lighten my load and experience the joy of life.

Fear to *faith*

In Science of Mind, we are taught that God does not withhold anything from us; it is we who restrict our good. The beliefs we cultivate from our family of origin, our culture and our life experiences influence our ability to receive from Spirit, so if we are experiencing lack in any area of our life, the way to change that is to change our beliefs. We were meant to live prosperous lives in all ways: perfect health, abundant wealth, loving relationships and unlimited creativity. If we open our minds up to thinking that we can have it all, then we will.

Today I welcome the flow of God's good into my life by aligning my beliefs with spiritual truth. Knowing that God gives unceasingly to me, I open up the inner floodgates of my mind so that I may experience good health, prosperity, loving relationships and creativity. This is my divine inheritance, and I claim it now.

Fear to *faith*

232

When I feel overwhelmed by the happenings of the world, I go to the home within my soul, and I find peace. This is the place where I commune with my spirit and God. Everyone has a home within them; and although everyone's home may be different, the feeling of comfort and ease is the same.

Something I like to teach people who have never entertained this concept is to create a vision board with images of what home means to them. Pictures of nature, animals and spiritual symbols are among the pictures I have seen people use. This allows us to have a visual representation of what our inner home is, and then it can become a part of us.

When the world outside feels uncomfortable, *I turn within to the home within my soul, and my faith is restored. I am spiritually nourished here, for this is where I find God.*

Fear to *faith*

I am always amazed by the power of consciousness. This morning I was grappling with the desire to know how something was going to unfold, and I got trapped in the stagnation of not knowing. We humans are not adept at patience and being comfortable with not knowing. When I remembered the truth that within the unknown is the known, I was able to return to peace knowing that all is being revealed in its right and perfect way and time. Suddenly I was set free, and I was able to relax as I realized that on the heels of not knowing, the knowing comes through.

Within the unknown is the known; within the uncertain is the certain. I live in the awareness that everything is in constant motion; nothing is ever stuck, and all answers are revealed when I remain open.

234

I believe in divine intervention, and I have faith that in the midst of all that is unfolding in our world that love and peace will prevail. Even though I may see disturbing patterns, I know there is a Higher Power that governs all life. Through Its ways and means, those patterns are broken apart, and good will be made manifest in ways our little minds cannot foresee. It is all about trusting in the ever-changing nature of life as Spirit shows up in ways that bring wholeness, love and peace into visible form in our world.

Today I lean into the power of God, and I trust that It is restoring balance and peace to our world. I know that It is intervening in Its own way, and I have faith that positive changes are unfolding.

Fear to *faith*

When I was meditating this morning, I realized I need to open up to receive the power and energy of God. Even though we are always connected to Spirit, we may not always feel connected to It. When we don't feel connected, we close ourselves off from Its guidance and support.

To reconnect with God, we must recognize Its presence and invite It to fill us up with peace, joy and love. We must consciously become the receivers of God's divine life force.

Today I open myself up to receive the energy of God, and I am instantly restored to a harmonious state of being. I feel divinely activated by Spirit's love and grace, and I move through my day with deep peace.

_____

_____

_____

_____

_____

_____

_____

_____

_____

_____

Fear to *faith*

236

I would like to share a mantra that came to me a couple of days ago that has brought me great joy. The mantra is: "God takes really good care of me." I believe that God is the source of all life and gives to us unceasingly. When we have this belief, we see Spirit show up in so many different ways in our lives and through a variety of channels. Feelings of lack and limitation disappear when we trust that God will always provide us with what we need.

Today I experience peace and serenity for I see how God takes really good care of me. All my needs are met, and I am relaxed as I take in the splendor of this day.

Fear to *faith*

Our vision is so much bigger than we think. Even when our attention may be focused on fear, outside of that focus lies a larger reality that dissolves all fear, and that reality is Spirit. All of us have the ability to radically expand our human experience and get unstuck from any fear that robs us of our happiness. When we open our eyes and look beyond fear and uncertainty, all stress is alleviated, and faith is restored.

Today I see beyond fear, and I behold the vast reality of Spirit that fills me with love and peace. This is where I keep my vision focused, and my life unfolds with grace and ease.

Fear to *faith*

238

I enjoy the human experience and being engaged with what is going on around me. However, when things shift and change in the world, I find that I get stuck in what I call the mosh pit of the collective energy that is agitated by what we are collectively seeing. When I am trapped in this limited perception, I aim my vision higher, and my view is vastly improved. I can see beyond the human drama and embrace the potential that is of God.

Today I aim my thoughts to a higher place where Spirit's love and peace reside. My mind is instantly balanced as harmony returns to my soul.

The metaphor of the bridge is powerful. Often we may feel like there is a huge chasm that separates us from where we would like to be in life or what we would like to experience. The remedy is to build a bridge of faith that connects us with the belief that we are moving forward into that which we want to experience in life. Whether it is health, a relationship or peace, we can build a bridge to anything.

Today I build a bridge of faith *that unites me with my good. I know that God is the ultimate bridge that connects me with the life I am ready to live.*

Fear to *faith*

240

Many of us live busy, distracted lives, and we don't take time to just be still. There is so much restoration that comes from setting aside lists, errands and things we "have to do," and allowing ourselves to just do nothing. Even if it is just for 5 or 10 minutes, when we break the current of energy that binds us to obligations, we free up that energy. We can then use it to recharge ourselves.

Today I give myself permission to be still and enjoy unstructured time. I am refreshed and rejuvenated when I sit in stillness, and I feel so much better.

_____

_____

_____

_____

_____

_____

_____

_____

_____

_____

Fear to *faith*

This morning I was reminded about the importance of cultivating the ability to spiritually live above our circumstances, no matter what is going on in our lives. One of my strategies for doing so is creating a place within my mind where I can find refuge from the outer world and experience peace and stillness. Even if I spend just 5 minutes a day in this sacred place, I am much more calm and present.

Within my mind lies a peaceful place *where spiritual nourishment is plentiful. When I go to this place to calm my spirit, my life is peaceful and serene, regardless of what is going on in the world.*

242

I have heard it said that the truth is always in plain sight; it is we who do not want to see it. There are so many questions I would like answered, but I know they won't be answered by a source outside of me. I believe that all the answers we are seeking are within us, so when we are yearning for truth, we just need to open our eyes and be receptive to seeing it.

I open my eyes to see the truth, *and all my questions are answered. I am grateful I have the awareness that all the wisdom of the universe lies within me, and it is there for me to know whenever I am ready to see it.*

Fear to *faith*

At any moment of any day, we can start fresh and set the tone for our life by virtue of our intention. I like to begin by setting the intention to be loving and kind toward myself and others. By keeping our consciousness in a state of love and kindness, we create peace and joy within ourselves, and that energy goes out into the world and impacts others.

I set my intention to be kind and loving toward all beings, including myself. I soften my heart and see the good in all people and all situations, and I am set free to live in harmony. Knowing that Spirit governs all through love and law, I trust that my world and the world at large is in good hands.

_____

_____

_____

_____

_____

_____

_____

_____

_____

_____

_____

_____

Fear to *faith*

244

The images that cross our visual field in a given day have more influence on us than we may know. I recently became present to the reality that the imbalance of women to men in leadership positions deeply affects our minds. The absence of the feminine in that which controls our country — and the world — sends a signal to our brains that it is not important, valued or needed.

This awareness is our call to remind ourselves of how vital feminine energy is to our world, and we must consciously counterbalance the images that cross our minds.

Today I recognize the importance of feminine energy, and I see its value in myself and in the world. I allow that energy to be expressed through me as strength, kindness, beauty and grace, knowing that when I acknowledge the feminine within me, it grows in the world.

Fear to *faith*

Recently, I experienced fear around the atrocities that continue to happen in our world. As I sat with my feelings, I realized that fear isn't just about what is before us. When we experience fear, we activate all the pre-existing fear that lurks in the subconscious region of our minds. All of our personal fears and the collective fears of humanity come to life, and before you know it, we are paralyzed. The good news is that awareness of this phenomenon restores our power and shrinks our fear to nothing.

Should fear arise within me, it quickly fades when I stay present to God's unyielding ability to bring peace, love and balance to all that is.

Fear to *faith*

246

There is so much beyond what is in front of us. Emma Curtis Hopkins encouraged people to look up when they are feeling out of sorts. When we look up, we see the vast universe in which we live, and we are reminded there is more than this planet and our problems in the scheme of life. Also, when we look up, we acknowledge a power higher than ourselves — Spirit — and It governs everything through order and law.

Today I look up and see how grand life is *as I see beyond that which is in front of me. I trust in the infinite power of God to bring peace, knowing that It creates balance in the universe in ways that are beyond my understanding.*

Even though we may feel powerless over the events of our world, there is something we can do spiritually to affect change. We can hold the High Watch. The High Watch means we use our consciousness to be the overseer of good demonstrating in our world. We do this by raising our consciousness to a place of knowing that all good is unfolding, regardless of appearances. It is to be the eyes of Spirit with love and kindness. And to have unwavering faith in the power of God to make all things right and harmonious in the midst of that which is unsettling. We must never underestimate the power of our consciousness to influence our world.

Today I hold the High Watch and stand firm in my faith that God's love and grace are unfolding through divine order and action, bringing peace to all. I don't have to know how this is happening; I just know it is.

248

Recently I went hiking in the local canyons with a wonderful group of women. Our tour guide told us there was a flood a few years ago that changed the look of the canyon. Gigantic boulders were moved, and to this day, you can still see dried mud on the towering palm trees and canyon walls.

We forget sometimes just how powerful water is. Spirituality is oftentimes symbolized by water, and I think this is fitting. It is easy to forget how powerful Spirit is in our lives because It is so subtle and gentle, but It is capable of transforming everything in our world.

As I stand in awe of the irrefutable power of Spirit, I know that when I surrender to Its flow, It carries me to the perfect places for me to live in peace, love and harmony.

_____

_____

_____

_____

_____

_____

_____

Fear to *faith*

I am a big believer in the power of our words. Today, in the collective consciousness that we all participate in, let us hold the word "peace" in our hearts. In our oneness, let us set the intention together that we believe peace can and will prevail in our world, and we will not allow ourselves to lose faith just because this peace has not yet fully manifested.

Today I have faith that the action of Spirit is working through all that is to bring peace to us individually and collectively.

250

I think our society encourages us to take sides. We have to be for this and against that. How about just being neutral? The definition of neutral is "not aligned with or supporting any side or position." Being neutral brings peace, and when you think about it, isn't God neutral? There is no judgment with God; everything just is what it is, for all is born of Spirit.

Today I keep my mind in a place of neutrality and center myself on peace. I walk through my day with a light heart as I take sides with nothing except God.

The God I believe in is everywhere present, within and around me, and It has given me free will to do as I please. The God I believe in does not intrude on my life, but It responds to my prayers and intentions. When I need Spirit's guidance, it is up to me to make the first move and invite It in to help me.

Today I call on the infinite power and presence of Spirit to reveal Itself in all ways, shapes and forms in my life. I know that when I make this request, Spirit shows up in the most amazing ways. Thank you, God, for blessing me so richly.

_____

_____

_____

_____

_____

_____

_____

_____

_____

_____

_____

_____

_____

_____

Fear to *faith*

252

Do you ever feel like there is something bothering you but you can't figure it out? Recently I had that experience. Something wasn't feeling quite right within me, and I couldn't understand what was going on. After deep contemplation, I realized I wasn't feeling loved. For a moment I questioned if that was really the answer to my quandary; I thought it had to be more complicated than that. No, it really was that simple. This insight led me to reflect on why I was not allowing myself to feel loved. Then I remembered that no matter what, that which created me, Spirit, loves me unconditionally 24/7.

Today I feel the love of Spirit through every part of my being, knowing I play an important role in this world. I share my love with everyone I interact with today, and that love spreads out to all.

Fear to *faith*

In Judaism, there is a custom of changing one's name if a person has been cured of an illness or achieved something big. The idea is that the person has shed their old identity, so they must receive a new name to symbolize their new identity. It's like the vibrational frequency of their old name no longer fits them.

I have learned that to change my life, I cannot be the same person I am now. I have to change myself to be a match for my new life. If I'm not living the life I desire, it is because I don't believe I can, and that is an identity issue.

I have all the strength and courage I need to change my identity so that I can be a vibrational match for the life I desire to live. I know that Spirit supports my transformation as I break free of all self-imposed limitations and embrace my expansion.

254

Sometimes I get so caught up in what is going on outside of myself that before I know it, I am totally locked out of the zone of peace that lies within me. I know so many people who are experiencing upheavals in their lives right now, and I can't help but be affected by what they are going through. However, I know that to truly help my loved ones, I must return to that serene place within that knows better. I must trust that Spirit's goodness is becoming visible, regardless of appearances.

I bathe myself in the inexhaustible pool of serenity that lies within my soul, and I am at peace. I have complete faith that life unfolds through Spirit's grace, and goodness is always the final outcome.

Each morning brings the gift of another day of life. Even though some mornings we may not be present to that sentiment, if we do some sort of spiritual practice before our day gets going, we can turn our attitude around. A spiritual practice does not have to be complicated. It can be as simple as reading an inspiring quote. Anything we do to center our thoughts on something positive will create a better day for us.

As I turn my attention to the Divine Light that dwells within me, my mind is cleansed, and my soul is refreshed. I welcome the day that is before me with optimism and faith, knowing my good is forever flowing into my life.

Fear to *faith*

256

Although it is natural for us to have expectations, we can experience feelings from disappointment to grief if those expectations are not met. When this happens, we are reminded that there is a bigger picture unfolding that our minds do not control. If we take a step back when experiencing disappointment and realize there is something better than we expected emerging, we free ourselves to receive that which is far superior to anything we imagined.

Today I let go of all expectations, *and I allow Spirit to express Its goodness in my life in ways that surprise and delight me.*

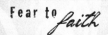

As a spiritually minded person skipping joyfully through the fields of life, there are times when I hit concrete. Then I have to make an uncomfortable decision that involves having a conversation that may upset someone. I so dread those moments, but I know I cannot ignore that action must be taken. What an incredible struggle between doing what I need to do for myself and not wanting confrontation. I can sit in the discomfort only so long, for I know that I must honor myself and do what I need to do, and just let the chips fall where they may.

Today I stand up for myself and courageously communicate anything that is on my heart to speak. I know that I can lean into Spirit for support and walk through any experience with a full and grateful heart.

_____

_____

_____

_____

_____

_____

_____

_____

Fear to *faith*

258

I believe there are times in life when we need to indulge ourselves and be lazy, and there are times when we need to be disciplined. Both are needed. When I feel spread too thin, I know I need to have some lazy time, and I absolutely love it. Too much structure calls for no structure so I can regain my balance. If, on the other hand, I need to make changes in my life because I am feeling stagnant, I know it is time for me to be disciplined so I can take myself to a higher level.

I maintain balance in my life for I know when to be still and when to be disciplined. Both are equally important for the evolution of my soul.

Fear to *faith*

I did it again! I got caught up in taking myself and life too seriously. This morning I got so weighed down by everything, that I finally cracked open and was able to hear Spirit say to me, "My dear, you are taking yourself and life much too seriously. This is all just consciousness, so change your consciousness, and you will find the humor in it all." Boy, that Spirit is so smart! The truth really does set us free.

My heart is lightened as I see the humor in life. I know that nothing needs to be taken too seriously, for all of life is governed by infinite intelligence, and Spirit's goodness always triumphs.

Fear to *faith*

260

I saw a wonderful movie called "Dying to Know." The movie focuses on the friendship between Ram Dass and Timothy Leary. Building on that relationship, the movie is filled with an abundance of great wisdom.

Something that stood out for me is a comment Ram Dass made about the importance of identifying with our soul. Most of us have a strong attachment to who we are in this lifetime — our history, our experiences, our path. However, this life we live is transitory, and our attachment to it creates fear because we know it will not last forever.

Identifying with who we are at the soul level diminishes our fear because we attach to the eternal nature of our being, and that goes on forever.

As I identify with my soul, I relax in the comfort of knowing there is a greater life beyond the one I am currently living. I enjoy this human experience with the understanding that I am more than it is.

Regardless of the relationship we had with our mother, the mother archetype is a powerful force in our psyche. To be whole beings, it is vitally important that we cultivate the ability to recognize and honor the mother within each of us. We all have the capacity to be a mother to ourselves.

During these strange times we live in, it is vitally important for us to find the maternal heart of our soul so we can draw on the love that does not judge; the love that is unquestioning; the love that is inexhaustible; the love we deserve.

Today I connect with the maternal nature of Spirit within me, and I fill myself up with Its unconditional love. My heart returns to a state of wholeness as I allow the mother within to nurture my soul.

262

I find it fascinating how much takes place in my mind from the time I center myself in the morning to when I finish my day. My mental energy gets pulled in so many different directions; before I know it, I am all over the place. When this happens, I close my eyes and imagine myself gathering all the energy that has been scattered to-and-fro, and I bring it back into the center of my being. This dissolves all chaos and restores my inner peace.

I maintain a calm and peaceful mind as I manage my mental energy with a watchful eye. I am able to easily bring my energy back to center whenever I get too distracted.

When I was a teenager, I had a close friend who had a challenging home life. In the early days of our friendship, she mentioned that she had a lot of problems, but at that time in my life, I didn't know what that meant. Even though I had my fair share of issues, I didn't have a mental concept of what it meant to live one's life anchored in problems, so it was foreign to me. As I look back on this, I see the wisdom of innocence. Although we cannot deny our challenges, we don't have to cement ourselves in them.

The transformative energy of Spirit is at the center of all challenges, bringing goodness to the surface. Knowing that no situation is fixed, I turn my attention to the Divine Perfection that is continually rising up and expressing Itself through all circumstances.

264

There was a time in my life when I would get really irritated if someone told me to "just let go" if I was going through a challenge. How could someone say that to me? Just let go? Really? Just like that?

Now this is advice I regularly give to people. There is only so much we can do when we are walking through difficult situations. There comes a time when we do need to let it go. Holding tightly to conditions and circumstances only constricts our receptivity to Spirit's guidance through difficult experiences.

Today I give myself the gift of letting go, and I am relieved of all burdens. I invite Spirit's grace into my experience to reveal the perfect resolution of all matters.

Fear to *faith*

If I were to say to you that you are the light of this world, would you reject that statement or would you accept it? We all have the ability to be the light of this world, but some days it can be challenging. Focusing on what is "wrong" in our lives or in the world causes our lights to dim. When we experience adversity, rather than allowing our lights to turn off, view this as a call to turn our lights on high.

Light clears away all darkness and allows us to be the light of this world. And God knows, our world needs all of us to be the light right now.

I see the light within me, and I shine it brightly. I know that my light contributes to the healing taking place in the world.

266

If we allow ourselves to become an empty vessel for Spirit to pour Itself into, we experience new life. When we open ourselves up to the Infinite Presence that is the great giver of life and let It fill us up, we can't go wrong. I know there are times when I want to figure everything out on my own, but when I empty my mind and let Spirit in, I receive ideas and direction that I never would have entertained using my own thinking.

Today I become an empty vessel, and I invite Spirit to pour Its love, wisdom and peace into my soul. I am refreshed, energized and ready for a powerful day.

Fear to *faith*

Setting priorities has become an important part of our daily lives. Many of us have a lot going on, and to maintain balance, we have to pick and choose what must be done each day and what can be done another day. In the past, I experienced a great deal of stress over my daily to-do list because I thought that everything had to be done on that day.

Now when I look at my daily list, as I go over each task, I ask myself, "Do I really need to do this today?" I find it liberating to watch my to-do list shrink when I think things through.

I take time to review all my daily tasks, and I create a day that is perfectly balanced. I manage my priorities with ease, always setting aside time for stillness.

Fear to *faith*

268

Forgiveness is a popular topic in spirituality. If we want to live happy and healthy lives, we have to forgive anyone we hold a grudge against.

In my own personal journey of forgiveness, I had to do a lot of work around forgiving my mom. When I was visiting her toward the end of her life, I had a powerful moment of self-reflection. As I looked at her, this feeling of love came over me, and I said to myself, "I hold nothing against you any longer."

I realized all the work I had done was finished. I also realized that forgiveness is a process, and it takes whatever time it takes for it to be complete.

I begin the process of forgiving anyone I am still holding a grudge against, knowing that doing so leads to inner freedom. Spirit guides me on this healing journey, and I gratefully let go of all that disrupts my inner peace.

Many people I know are waiting for their big breakthrough to take place. They have set their intention, completed the inner work and are chomping at the bit for their desired outcome to transpire. This is one of the most challenging places to be because our faith gets tested. We may ask God why it is taking so long. Why do I have to wait one moment longer? I am tired of living in this condition.

There are a lot of things we do not know about that contribute to our demonstrations, so we must surrender to the mind of God and trust that It has it all figured out.

I know that Spirit is doing the work to bring forth my demonstration even though my mind cannot see it, so I relax in a state of open receptivity, knowing my breakthrough is unfolding in the perfect way and at the perfect time.

270

This life requires us to be engaged in so many different realities on any given day. There is the reality of our home life, the reality of work, the reality of driving the car. Present within all realities is Spirit, but we many not acknowledge that or see that because we are so focused on whatever reality we are participating in.

A new spiritual practice I have begun reconnects me to Spirit during my day, based on my taking responsibility for putting up the wall that blocks me from seeing God — and then tearing that wall down. I thought I would share it with you so you can try it out yourself.

There are only three steps. The first step is to tell yourself to take down the wall you built that is blocking you from seeing Spirit. The second step is to realize that God is standing right in front of you — and always is. (Yes, I know God is within, but this is a visual exercise for the purpose of stimulating reconnection.) The third step is letting God's energy fill you up with peace, joy and love.

I consciously tear down all the walls I have built that separate me from Spirit, and I am rejuvenated by Its healing presence.

Many of us have been taught to live life under linear rules. Everything must unfold as it always has. However, this type of thinking is losing its grip on us. More and more people are coming to the realization that linear thinking is not the absolute. Instead of accepting limited thinking and saying "I can't" when we have a dream or an idea that may not be supported by the masses, it is time to say, "Why not?" It is time for us to be open to embracing the universe of vast possibilities and allow new realities to become our reality.

Today I open my mind *to the infinite universe of possibilities as I embrace that which is calling me to live a bigger life.*

272

Two of the most powerful words in our language are "thank you." It feels good to say them, and it feels good to receive them. We have been given the gift of life and so many other wonderful things, we could be saying "thank you" all day for all that we have.

Whenever I get stuck in a thought that is uncomfortable, I stop and say those two simple words, "thank you," and I am filled with peace and joy. God knows, there is always something I can be thankful for.

Today I say "thank you" for everything in my life, knowing that Spirit blesses me with endless gifts.

Fear to *faith*

This morning, Spirit got my attention in the most amazing way. After I got out of the shower, my iPad mysteriously started playing music. The song it selected was "Love Comes Tumbling Down" by U2, and the part of the song that was playing was clearly my post for the day: "All roads lead to where you are."

Speaking for myself and countless people I have spoken to over the years, at some time in our lives we have contemplated where would be if we had made different choices. Would things have turned out better? This is an exercise in futility, because we really don't know if our lives would have been better had we made different choices. We are where we are, here and now, and that is a good thing.

Within us lies all the power of the universe to create goodness no matter what preceded us. We have the unlimited life of Spirit ready and willing to move us forward in whatever direction we choose. So while all roads led us to where we are today, we have unlimited possibilities stretched out before us. How cool is that?

I honor the path that brought me to where I am today, knowing that all the goodness of the universe lies before me. I trust myself to make wonderful choices that move me forward.

Fear to *faith*

274

Every now and then, the words from the Fleetwood Mac song "Landslide" settle into my mind for contemplation: "Can I sail through the changin' ocean tides? Can I handle the seasons of my life?"

At first, I'll look outside of myself and think about how our culture portrays aging, and I get a little nervous. As I go deeper, I move into a place of spiritual truth, and I realize I don't have to age as society dictates. I can do it my way because my thoughts and choices create my reality.

So the answer is yes, I can handle the seasons of my life, because I choose to live each season to the fullest, and the universe completely supports me in that intention.

I joyfully move through each season of life knowing I am in charge of creating my experience.

Fear to *faith*

One of my favorite ways to shift my consciousness is through visualization. Pictures exert great power over us. We can change our experience simply by looking at a picture that represents how we want to feel. For me, any picture that represents freedom is always a great go-to visualization. I believe that when we are in an inner state of freedom, we are knowing that all is possible, and we can unchain ourselves from whatever it is we no longer wish to experience.

I visually connect with that which represents how I desire to feel, and my whole consciousness changes for the better.

Fear to *faith*

I talk a lot about going to God to receive support, love and direction. This morning I was thinking about that, and I realized that maybe those words don't make sense to other people. For me, the first thing I do when I go to God is I turn off my mind, move my awareness to my heart and I surrender my need to control everything — how things are to unfold, what the outcomes are going to look like, etc.

Next, I get quiet. Really quiet. I shift my energy from thinking and doing to being and receiving. I am then able to feel my oneness with that which is bigger than me, Spirit, and I lean into Its wisdom and light.

Last, I allow myself to be the child of Spirit, the recipient of Its goodness, and I experience deep peace. This to me is going to God.

I stop trying to make everything work in my life, and I go to God. I allow Spirit to show me the way and give me the direction to follow for my good to unfold in the most amazing ways.

It is so easy to get stuck in the same old routines. We go to the same places to eat. We drive the same routes to our frequent destinations. We have our daily routines, and the list goes on.

Whenever I start to feel bored or stuck in my life, I know it is time for me to try something new to break the monotony of my worn-out habits. It is really positive for us to change our habits and do things differently. Science has even proven that our brain health improves when we try new things. The cool thing is that the newness doesn't have to be radical. Just changing a habit or two will bring freshness into our lives.

Today I choose to do at least one thing differently, and I am totally revitalized. I invite new experiences into my life that enliven me and connect me to the excitement of being alive.

278

The attributes of God are wonderful words for us to focus on when setting the state of consciousness that we wish to experience. Normally I choose peace or love, but today I thought it would be lovely to experience beauty. In my mind, beauty is beyond the physical definition of the word; it is a state of mind where harmony and grace are perceived by all of the senses. It is a consciousness that enables us to be detached from linear thought and relax into the boundless nature of Spirit as It expresses through all life.

A consciousness steeped in Spirit's beauty allows us to see the divine pattern woven within everything and everyone.

As I tune into the beauty of Spirit, my consciousness is raised to a higher frequency that is congruent with divine harmony. I can now experience the beauty of life that forever surrounds me.

Fear to *faith*

Today I find myself having to stand on my principles and make a decision that could ruffle the feathers of others. My parents taught me the importance of speaking up when you see injustice or unethical behavior, and that is woven into the fabric of my being. However, I still feel fear when I know I need to stand up and speak up. So what do I do? I lean into Spirit in a big way, and I pray. In my mind, standing on principle is one of the most spiritual things we can do. We are truly allowing ourselves to stand in righteousness and faith and express the higher wisdom of our soul that is in alignment with integrity.

I trust in the Infinite Wisdom that resides within my soul to guide me rightly and support me in standing on my principles. I know that God's light is shining from within me when I speak from a place of truth and integrity.

Fear to *faith*

280

When Spirit puts something on our heart to do and our passion is ignited, we must take action. We have to hitch our horses to our wagon and "giddy up." As I walk through this myself right now, I am filled with apprehension and doubt. Can I really do this? Do I have the energy? Who am I to think I can drive this passion into manifestation?

Thank God the energy of passion is so much stronger than fear. Whenever those fears and insecurities pop up, I remember that my passion is rooted in Spirit, and the fear dissolves, allowing me to do what is mine to do.

I have complete faith that Spirit gives me the power, energy and drive to follow my passions to their complete fulfillment.

Fear to faith

It is a fact of life that growing can be uncomfortable. Growing pains certainly aren't reserved just for children.

Today I am taking a big step in my personal growth by speaking up in front of a group of people and addressing something I see as unethical. I am nervous about doing this, and I have even thought about taking the easy road, saying nothing.

However, that still small voice, Spirit, tells me this is mine to do, and I have all the strength of the universe supporting me. This is a reminder to all of us that we should never cower to feelings of discomfort when we need to speak up.

Today I speak my truth, and regardless of the outcome, I know I am doing what Spirit has given me to do to be of highest service.

282

During a processing group I led yesterday, the talking piece we used — a selenite heart — slipped out of my hands and onto the floor, where it broke in two. There was a collective gasp as we all stared at the broken heart lying on the floor. All of our minds were seeing meaning in what had just happened.

As I looked at the two pieces of the broken heart, I noticed that one piece was much bigger than the other, and I saw this as the truth about losing that which we love. The larger piece of the heart represents the joy we feel toward that object of love, and the smaller piece is the sadness we experience when that love is no longer in our life. After our healing is complete around loss, our joy is much more powerful than our sorrow.

*I **know** that the experience of heartbreak opens me up to a deeper level of love, as I allow Spirit's grace to restore me to wholeness.*

Fear to *faith*

I was recently charged up and focused on standing in my truth and making decisions that were uncomfortable. Now that I am on the other side of all that, I realize how fixated I was on what I was experiencing and how I was living in what I call "red energy." I was feeling fierce and maybe a little pissed off. However, it was important for me to experience all that discomfort so I could do what I needed to do.

Many people in the spiritual community have the misconception that one of the goals of spiritual practice is to avoid and escape uncomfortable feelings. This is spiritual bypass, and it creates a divide within ourselves because it denies our humanity. To spiritually evolve, we must embrace all of our feelings and walk through them, not around them.

I honor every feeling I experience, knowing it brings me to a greater understanding of myself and moves me forward. Spirit provides me with all the strength I need to work through any emotion I experience.

284

Three of the most powerful words ever proclaimed are, "Let freedom ring." Freedom is our natural birthright, and we are so blessed to live in a country that recognizes that.

Even though we all want freedom, do you feel completely free? I know for myself that there are times when I feel like I am in bondage to the past, false beliefs and limited thinking. So today I choose to liberate myself from anything that stands in the way of my complete freedom. I use my awareness to unlock any mental chains that keep me from enjoying the freedom that is my natural birthright.

Today I celebrate the freedom of being that is Spirit's gift to me. I am able to free myself of any bondage I still live in so I may experience freedom in all areas of my life.

Fear to *faith*

Last night I was listening to a guided meditation, and one of the last sentences of the mediation is, "Awaken your inner alchemist." Alchemy is the ancient art of transforming elements into something completely different, such as lead into gold.

In our time, alchemy is often used as a metaphor for personal transformation, as it is used in the meditation I mentioned. The big "aha" I wanted to share with you is as I go through my own personal transformation, there are times when I just don't know where to begin or what to do. The idea of handing off the "how" of inner change to another aspect of myself that knows how to do it — the inner alchemist — brings me great peace.

By activating my inner alchemist, my little mind doesn't have to figure things out. I know the alchemist within me will set everything in motion for my transformation to unfold.

I awaken my inner alchemist to assist me with my personal transformation, as Spirit paves the way for my new path to be revealed.

286

I know this might sound insane, but I think it is an idea worth contemplating. I think many of us have an unconscious need to punish ourselves, and this has an effect on our life experiences. The subconscious part of us is a repository of all of our experiences and the collective beliefs of our society. If we have not examined the mental and emotional programming that was instilled in us, an unconscious part of us may be holding onto guilt that was not processed when it was developing in us.

Becoming aware of how we may be punishing ourselves is not easy, but it can be done, and it is worth the effort. If there is anything happening to you in your life that you don't like, ask yourself if this experience is serving as some sort of punishment you unconsciously think you deserve. Your answer may be "no," but it is certainly worth asking, especially if it leads to a realization that changes your life for the better.

I have the courage to see that which has been hidden in my subconscious mind so that I can become aware of any self-punishing beliefs that have been controlling my destiny. Knowing that Spirit loves me unconditionally, I, too, love myself unconditionally as I release all thoughts that do not support that love.

Fear to *faith*

I had the pleasure of experiencing a crystal bowl meditation with a group of people. We were all moved into a totally different state of consciousness, as if the vibration of the bowl rearranged the cells of our bodies and our minds, restoring us to a place of tranquility.

As I contemplate this experience today, I realize how I can get trapped in whatever is currently on my mind and fixate on that until there is some sort of movement or resolution. The bowl experience reminded me that there are things I can do to break up the energy holding me in a place of stress or impatience so that I can relax into the flow of the unfolding of my life.

Knowing that my life is governed by the mind of God, I am filled with peace and serenity as I trust that all is unfolding in its right and perfect way.

288

Becoming aware of what we are allowing to influence our energy is vitally important for managing inner peace. There are so many sources to consider: the world at large, family, friends and our own consciousness. When I am feeling out of sorts, this is my signal that I need to take an energy inventory. What am I plugging into that needs to be unplugged? When I figure that out, I plug into Spirit.

Having an energy that is pure, clean and most powerful to connect with, such as God, neutralizes my energy and puts me in a balanced state of optimism and peace.

My soul is refreshed and my mind is cleared out when I turn to Spirit's loving presence. I am now returned to my natural state of balance and serenity.

Fear to *faith*

On the road to personal transformation, there is so much work we do to be self-aware and change our thinking. Today I am reminded that we also need to reach for a higher level of excellence in our lives. Mediocrity is not living life. Aspiring toward a greater, more fulfilling life experience is truly our purpose.

Knowing that I have the ability to take my life to new heights, I embrace the Divine within me as It leads me to a greater path for me to walk upon.

Fear to *faith*

290

Looking underneath the surface of our consciousness is a must for those of us who desire greater inner peace. I recently found myself going into judgment about someone, and I couldn't let it go. After indulging in that mental state for far too long, I felt so awful inside of myself that I was finally able to stop the current of thought I was in and look underneath the surface.

I discovered that I was judging this person because they disappointed me, and that made me sad. The judgment was preventing me from going into sadness, which is what I needed to feel in order to move on. When I found that buried treasure, everything changed within me. I felt relieved that I had discovered the cause of what was really bothering me, allowing me to feel what I truly needed to feel so I could be free.

I feel safe going beneath the surface of my consciousness so I can feel whatever I need to feel to process my experiences. Spirit provides me with the strength to see whatever I need to see so I can return to a place of peace.

_____

_____

_____

_____

Fear to *faith*

Wouldn't life be easier if there were some book or app we could access to get all the answers when life gets sticky, tough decisions need to be made, and we don't know what to do? Well, there is such a resource — your heart — and your heart is connected to the greatest source of wisdom there is — God. Whenever we face challenging situations that require big decisions, we have to go to our heart and make sure no stone lies unturned. We have to feel as confident as we can that we have done everything in our power to resolve the situation so we can have the confidence we did what was right and not feel any regret. The heart knows all.

I turn to my heart to guide me rightly through all life situations knowing my heart is eternally connected to Spirit's wisdom. I have clarity and focus as all decisions fall into place for the highest and best good to unfold.

_____

_____

_____

_____

_____

_____

Fear to *faith*

292

Even though we have complete authority over our state of consciousness, when we are walking through discomfort, we may forget that. Strong feelings of anxiety, upset or anger can be so overwhelming that we lose sight of our ability to shift our consciousness into a different state of being.

Today I give you a tool to use to remind you of your power to shift your consciousness when you are mired in uncomfortable feelings. That tool is your inner shift key. Just press it with your mind's eye, and your energy will begin moving in a new direction.

I recognize that I am the master of my consciousness, and I can shift my state of being at any time simply by declaring that I am ready to feel differently.

Fear to *faith*

It seems like so many of us are moving through major challenges right now, and we are getting stuck in fear. Focusing on worst case scenarios and feeling like we have no control can paralyze us. This is our call to Spirit. It is time to shake ourselves free and raise our thoughts up to see the positive possibilities that are always present and give Spirit a chance to bring new options to the table. It is our responsibility to call this forth and create the space for a new positive direction to present itself to us. God always delivers when we ask.

I turn to Spirit to bring forth new ideas that shift the direction of my life for the better. I can change any circumstance through my conscious recognition of Spirit's power to bring a positive outcome to anything I experience.

_____

_____

_____

_____

_____

_____

294

Music is so incredibly powerful. Today I heard a song I hadn't heard in such a long time, and it evoked a feeling I hadn't felt in decades. Just listening to the melody awakened a feeling of vibrancy, excitement and fearlessness within me because it touched a place inside me that is from my youth.

I realized there has been an energy missing from my consciousness that sustains my youthful spirit, and I am so grateful I found it and can weave it back into my present state of mind.

My spirit is moved by the music of the universe as it expresses in this time and space. I am lifted up by melodies that bring peace, love, joy and harmony into my life, knowing this is one way God speaks to me.

_____

_____

_____

_____

_____

_____

_____

_____

Fear to *faith*

There are endless opportunities presented to us each day for deep contemplation and meditation. One of my favorite things to do is use my routine household chores as symbolic rituals to shift my consciousness. For example, when I am sweeping the floor, I think about sweeping out all the little things that are cluttering my mind so that I can have clarity. When I wash the dishes, I see the water as washing away all that is not serving me. This is a great way to change the experience of housekeeping and bring more spiritual practice into our everyday lives.

I see mundane tasks as opportunities to deepen my spirituality and my connection to God.

296

We are so blessed to live in a time where we have a vast array of healing modalities available to us to improve our health. There is everything from traditional Western medicine to energy healing. In the midst of all these external healing modalities, there is one I believe we underutilize, and that is the power of the body to correct itself should we experience imbalance. If we cultivate a daily practice of consciously recognizing our body's ability to heal itself through its own innate intelligence, then perhaps we could prevent many of the illnesses that plague our world.

Today and every day, I recognize the Infinite *Intelligence that governs my body's systems, knowing there is an inner healing power that is always active within me.*

Sometimes we forget that we have the power to shift our state of being by making a different choice in what we are feeling. This is particularly true of fear. Fear is such a strong emotion, and because there is a huge survival component to it, it can feel impossible to shift out of it. However, our minds are much stronger than any feeling, and we have the ability to change our inner experience simply by knowing that we can, and by choosing a different thought and feeling.

Instead of just allowing ourselves to languish and suffer in uncomfortable emotions, we can move our thought in a different direction and change our feeling state. We can do this by introducing a new thought into our minds. If I feel fear, all I need to say is something like, "Love is all there is," and my mind moves in a totally new direction, into a new feeling state, and I feel much better.

God has given us a flexible mind, and it serves us to learn how to use it affirmatively so we can live peaceful lives.

Today I choose faith over fear, and I relax into the flow of this abundant life Spirit has given me to live. I am the master of my consciousness, and I use my intention to create and maintain a joyful state of being.

Fear to *faith*

Sometimes it seems as though the whole world is going mad, as violence erupts with no end in sight. When I see this happening, I call on God in a big way. When I feel fear over unnecessary war-mongering rhetoric, when I get upset at the reminder that so many people do not see hate as a call to look within but instead see it as a call to destroy others, I know I have work to do.

It is clear that I am being called to remember who is really in charge and how my consciousness contributes to the healing that is before us. I don't know how this is all going to work out, but I know it will. If I choose to center myself in peace and love, I am contributing to the calming of the collective energy that has been stirred up.

As I turn to the endless reservoir of love and peace that lies within me, I experience tranquility. I trust in the harmonizing power of the universe to bring peace to all.

When I was meditating on what I would write today, the image of the hero and heroine standing at the bow of the ship from the movie "Titanic" popped into my mind. The more I contemplated that image, the more I realized that it is the perfect symbol of faith. Sometimes we may feel like we are traveling on the Titanic, but we must step out onto the front of the ship, fully open and receptive to what lies on the horizon — which is unlimited possibility — and know that Spirit securely holds us.

We have nothing to fear when we trust that Spirit is always with us. When we keep our gaze forward instead of dwelling on fear, we will arrive safely at our destination.

I keep my vision focused on the horizon of good that lies before me, knowing that my life is in Spirit's loving hands.

_____

_____

_____

_____

_____

_____

_____

_____

Fear to *faith*

300

Water is a powerful symbol of purification, and today I am drawn to invoke that symbol to purify my consciousness. This has been a week filled with murky imagery, and today is the day I choose to cleanse my mind and start fresh.

I am so grateful that Spirit has given us the ability to clear our minds so we don't have to get trapped by dark thoughts. We can do this through meditation, being in nature or just shifting our focus. So I invite you to join me today in cleansing our minds of muddy thoughts and filling ourselves up with pure thoughts of love, peace, forgiveness and unity.

I call forth the loving energy of Spirit to cleanse my mind of all that does not reflect Its love and peace, and I am free to live this day with a grateful and loving heart.

_____

_____

_____

_____

_____

_____

_____

Fear to *faith*

When undertaking deep spiritual work, we are often asked the question, "Who are you?" We might start by answering that we are our history — our family, experiences, relationships. Then we may say we are our careers, our hobbies, our life roles. However, none of these are the right answer, because who we really are cannot be defined in human terms.

We are made of the divine substance of Spirit, and we are more than our human minds can conceive. We are love, light and energy that has no form. Yet through our consciousness, we call it all into form and make it our own until we grow out of it and start all over again.

My answer to the question, "Who are you?", is I am everything and nothing.

I no longer see myself as a fixed and finite person but as boundless spiritual energy that can create whatever I choose to be and experience in this life.

_____

_____

_____

_____

_____

_____

_____

Fear to *faith*

302

To aid us in our quest to improve our lives, many teachers encourage us to use the technique of visualization. The idea is that if you can visualize exactly what you want your life to look like, you activate the universal energy to produce it.

While I see merit in this approach, I believe it is imperative for us to engage our hearts in creating the life we desire as well. The heart is an extremely strong energy field, and when we are vibrating with the feeling we most desire to experience in our life, we draw the form of what represents that feeling into our experience. We tap into a far greater field of infinite possibilities through our vibration than we do by outlining our desires through the limits of our minds' eyes.

I tune into the feeling state of my ideal life, and the universe responds by filling my life up with all that mirrors that feeling.

Fear to *faith*

The life of Princess Diana offers a huge lesson for all of us. As I contemplate her life, the phrase that pops into my mind is "all that glitters is not gold." On the outside, Princess Diana appeared to have everything, but in reality she had nothing because she turned her back on her heart. Just days before her wedding to Prince Charles, she told her sister she wanted to back out, but her sister said it was too late. She had to go through with it. She sacrificed her happiness and her life because she didn't want to disappoint anyone.

I think Princess Diana's story is a cautionary tale for us all to never compromise our happiness for the sake of sparing upset to others or causing them an inconvenience.

I follow my heart's urgings, *knowing it always guides me toward a life that is happy and free.*

_____

_____

_____

_____

_____

_____

Fear to *faith*

When I was struggling to figure out what to say at a celebration of life for a client who made his transition, I reached out to his spirit and asked for some help. He said to me, "Just paint a picture of the time we spent together and what that meant to you." That was just the guidance I needed.

His advice got me thinking about how our minds are like galleries filled with paintings of our life experiences, and we can stroll around at any time and look at where we have been and all we have done. The unusual thing about our mental gallery is that we can make changes to the paintings as our perception of our past changes. What may have once been an ugly painting can become a beautiful masterpiece with a few additional brushstrokes of love and forgiveness.

I am grateful for all I have experienced in my life and my ability to transform the past by changing my thought.

The feeling of completion is incredibly gratifying. We have many different things going on in our lives that are in process. When one is completed, it is so liberating. Whether we finished a concrete project or came full circle about something we felt incomplete about, or when something is done and we can let it go from our energy field, it is wonderful. I love the feeling of completion because it gives me a sense of accomplishment and moves me forward. I also know it means I am ready for something new, so I set my intention to make sure that newness is really good.

Today I celebrate all that is complete in my life, as I welcome new, positive experiences. Life is a never-ending circle, and I am grateful Spirit guides me through it all.

306

To live a life of happiness and freedom, we must become aware of the thoughts and beliefs lodged in our subconscious that weigh us down. Many of us are carrying around beliefs about ourselves that are destructive, but we don't know it. If we feel disappointed in ourselves or our lives feel stuck, chances are there is something underneath the surface of our conscious awareness that needs to be revealed and healed. When we bring these old beliefs to the surface and counter them with the truth about who we are, they can't paralyze us anymore, and we can live a peaceful life.

I am ready to let go of beliefs that do not reflect the divine magnificence of my soul, and I am free to live a life of unlimited joy, peace and abundance.

_____

_____

_____

_____

_____

_____

_____

_____

Fear to *faith*

When I was a child, it was a big deal in our family when we celebrated the High Holidays. We all got together, went to temple and celebrated with a big family dinner. Those days are long gone, as is my family. I always feel a twinge of sadness during the holidays for what no longer is. Some people have suggested I go to temple to temper those feelings; however, that never works.

I have come to realize that although those memories are precious to me, I can't bring that time of my life and my family back. Today I enjoy a big soul family of friends I am deeply connected to, and even though we don't share the same DNA, we share the same spirit.

I honor my family of origin as I recognize that my true family goes far beyond those who raised me. My family is all of Spirit's creations, and I am never alone.

308

After a week of being intensely focused, today I purposely chose to be unfocused and to surrender to the current of life as it unfolds for me. I think it is healthy for us to take a break from thinking we need to direct the traffic of our life. It is so rejuvenating just to float in our own energy stream and be present to the life that surrounds us without having to control it all.

I am grateful for the moments of tranquility that come as I take time to just be and observe the beauty of life.

Fear to *faith*

The power of any collective consciousness cannot be underestimated, especially when it is grounded in a spiritual attribute such as peace. I am a firm believer that our world can become more peaceful through a collective intention of knowing that world peace is becoming a reality. I leave the "how it will unfold" to Spirit. When I see war-mongering rhetoric being bantered about, instead of feeling fear, I tell myself that there is another solution to this situation that is peaceful. Through my knowing, I open the door to the manifestation of that solution. The more of us that hold this intention, the quicker we will see peace in our world.

I know my thoughts are powerful, so I lean into Spirit and trust that world peace is emerging because I believe it can.

310

One thing we never lack for are distractions. There is always someone or something vying for our attention, and it is challenging not to get swept into the drama. We may even have the belief that we need to engage in the drama because we think it needs our energy and attention. However, this can cause us to ignore our own souls and the meaningful things we are going through in the depths of our being.

There is no hierarchy of importance regarding what each of us is dealing with inside the sacred space of our soul, and honoring that and paying attention to what is yearning to be expressed and processed is vitally important for our well-being.

Today I turn away from all distractions and embrace my own journey of evolution taking place within me.

_____

_____

_____

_____

_____

_____

_____

Fear to *faith*

One of my constant intentions is to live light as a feather. I find that the more I keep my mind clear and light, the easier it is to move through life and adjust to the many changes that happen throughout this Earth walk. This is definitely easier said than done because there is so much stuff that can weigh us down. This is where surrendering to Spirit comes in.

Whenever I feel like I am carrying too much mental or emotional weight, I surrender the heaviness to Spirit. I ask for guidance on how to resolve whatever is weighing me down, and the perfect answer is revealed.

Today I surrender any heaviness *I am carrying to Spirit, and my lightness of being is fully restored.*

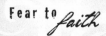

312

One of the most difficult concepts for us to understand when learning about spirituality is the idea that all beings are perfect, whole and complete. Many of us have been raised to think we are flawed and insufficient, and this idea is reinforced by society. But the truth is that we are perfect, whole and complete if we look at ourselves through Spirit's eyes rather than human eyes. When we stop defining perfection as complying to some external measurement and see it as something that we naturally are because we are creations of Spirit, then we can appreciate ourselves in a whole new light.

I am able to see myself as perfect, whole and complete for Spirit created me to be Its unique expression of Life. I appreciate myself and how I show up in this world, knowing that it is perfect.

Fear to *faith*

Recently when I was driving home from a long day of going non-stop from one place to the next, I was waiting at a red light, and I had a profound spiritual experience. As I sat there waiting for the light to change, I wasn't thinking about my challenges, my to-do list, my opinions or how I could change the world. All I felt was the light of Spirit filling me up with peace. Without even trying, I tuned out all distractions and experienced divine harmony. I was in awe of what I was experiencing and so grateful, because this is the state of mind that heals us. When the light turned green, I was ready to re-engage with my earthly life, but with a whole new attitude.

Today I open up to the mystical presence of Spirit to fill me up with love and harmony. My soul is refreshed as I experience the energy of Spirit that lives within my heart.

313

Fear to *faith*

314

In an attempt to relieve distressing inner dialogue, many of us run away by looking for distraction in the form of everything from TV to workaholism to drugs. The only way to tame the inner beast is to look at it, listen to it and soothe it. When we stand in our spirituality, these thoughts are powerless, and we can see them without being consumed by them. As we gain an understanding of where they have come from, they lose their power, and we can master our consciousness and our experience of this life.

When discordant thoughts arise within me, I see them without fear, knowing I am more powerful than they are. I am able to tame my mind by connecting with the Divine within me that reminds me of who I really am.

Immediately following a heavy experience, I find myself in a clearing field that allows me to process the experience. Even though I am grateful the experience is behind me, it is still fresh in my mind. I know I must be loving and compassionate toward myself as I review what took place and release it.

Sometimes I experience a lot of discomfort during this process. Oftentimes there comes a point when I have to admit how awful the experience was, but a part of me fights that feeling because I have been taught that we should see the good in all that happens in life. However, sometimes we cannot move forward in our processing if we do not allow ourselves to acknowledge those feelings.

I know that when I allow every feeling to emerge without resistance or judgment, I feel so much better, and I am able to move forward in freedom.

I no longer judge or deny any feelings I need to feel that facilitate my healing. Spirit has blessed me with a variety of feelings that allow me to release my emotional energy in a healthy manner.

Fear to *faith*

316

Words are incredibly powerful — so powerful, in fact, that they can shift our mood in a heartbeat. One of my favorite words is "kindness". Just saying the word melts my heart and soothes my soul. After all the emotional challenges I have experienced during the past couple of weeks, today I am parking my consciousness in kindness. I am going to embody it, live it, give it and experience it. And I am not going to just direct it externally; I am going to turn it inward on myself.

I invite you to join me in this intention so you can enjoy the beauty of life that surrounds you and is within you.

Today I bathe myself in kindness, and my world turns to gold. My heart is now open to express love to all beings and to myself, and I feel joyful and alive.

_____

_____

_____

_____

_____

_____

_____

Fear to *faith*

The game of American football is so rich with life lessons. The ball is symbolic of our dreams and goals, and the entire game is a metaphor for the journey we go through to achieve all we desire. There is an inner struggle that we sometimes experience when we are charging full speed ahead toward manifesting our goal and something blocks us from moving ahead. Those things can be doubts, insecurities or even impatience.

So what's a person to do? Keep running! Push the blocks away, and don't engage with them. When we focus on our goals and have no doubt we will achieve them, then nothing can stop us.

As I fully invest my energy into my goals and dreams, the universe takes care of how they are to unfold. My job is to keep the faith and keep moving forward.

_____

_____

_____

_____

_____

_____

_____

_____

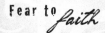

Fear to *faith*

318

Today I realized that underneath all the people, things and experiences I am grateful for is God. In Jewish tradition, Saturdays are considered the day of rest or Sabbath. This is the day we dedicate ourselves to reflect on the Creator of all life and Its never-ending gifts and blessings.

When I was a little girl, I learned that the more religious Jews could not do anything on the Sabbath — they could not drive, turn on lights, cook, etc. As a kid I thought, "What a bummer!" As an adult, I totally get it. The reason for the restrictions is so that people are not distracted by the doings of life so they can spend the whole day contemplating and connecting with Spirit. That is pretty cool.

Today I take the time to connect with Spirit in a substantial and meaningful way, and I see Its presence in all beings, all things and within myself. Thank you, Spirit, for this glorious life.

Fear to *faith*

For most of my life, I kept my body flexible. But within the last 5 years, I have not kept up with my stretches, and some of my muscles have become really tight. When I recently attempted to stretch those muscles, pain and stiffness arose. I lamented to myself about how flexible I used to be, and I gave up.

However, after I stopped feeling sorry for myself, I realized that I can regain my flexibility by stretching every day. So I made the commitment to do that, and as I felt the discomfort, I reminded myself that one day the pain would cease and my flexibility would return. When I was stretching this weekend, the pain was gone, and my flexibility improved. I am so grateful I kept at it even though I wasn't seeing immediate results.

I think this serves as a lesson for all of us to remember whenever we are stretching ourselves into new territory, whether it is spiritual, physical, emotional or vocational. It takes daily practice for us to loosen our restrictions and become flexible so we can grow into a new way of being in this world. The key is not to give up when we aren't seeing the results we want to see in the timeframe we think we should be seeing them. Keep stretching, because one day, you will be exactly where you want to be.

I take time every day to stretch myself into a more expansive way of living my life and becoming the person I am ready to be.

Fear to *faith*

320

Yesterday I saw someone I hadn't seen in a while. When she asked me how I was doing, I told her that everything was good. I was experiencing a lot of peace and stability in my life. Her response to me was unexpected; she said I had better enjoy it because it won't last forever. As you might imagine, I was totally taken aback by her words. I know she was coming from her own experience, but I felt uneasy because, for a brief moment, I took her words in as truth. I quickly reminded myself that that is her reality, not mine.

Even though I know that life is always changing, I am the master of my consciousness, and I can be peaceful and stable regardless of what is changing in my world.

There is only one authority of truth in my life, and that is Spirit. I trust myself to know what is true for me as I connect with the infinite wisdom that dwells within my soul for all my answers and guidance.

_____

_____

_____

_____

_____

Fear to *faith*

This morning when I felt a little fear come up, I heard this sweet voice say, "Fear not, little lamb," and my mind instantly returned to peace. This is a reminder of the power we have to shift our consciousness when we get stuck in fear or any uncomfortable state of being. The key is to choose a counter-feeling to restore our balance. If I feel fear, I go to the feeling of love. If I feel chaos, I go to peace. Our minds will follow us wherever we direct our thoughts to go, so the power to move ourselves out of discord and into peace is in our hands.

I use my consciousness to create a balanced state of being by choosing emotions that create peace in my mind.

Fear to *faith*

It brings me great comfort to know that beyond what I know and what I see in this life, there is so much more that exists. A change of thought and ideas is refreshing to the soul, and it allows us to stretch beyond the confines of beliefs and habits that may keep us stagnant or stuck in our lives.

Today I am giving a Hanukkah presentation, and I am reminded how my spiritual beliefs have radically expanded since I was a little girl and was not aware of other ways of seeing and experiencing God. I cannot imagine my life without the depth of understanding I have cultivated by seeing beyond what I was originally taught about Spirit.

I go outside of my human understanding of life, and I open up to the infinite knowledge of the universe. Everything changes for the better when I allow new ideas to open my eyes and see other ways of experiencing the greatness of life.

I recently was disappointed in myself because I thought I didn't do the best I could have done in a situation. As I was going down the rabbit hole, I felt so bad about myself that I thought I needed to endure some sort of punishment so that I would have a resolution. As I became the observer of my thoughts, I realized an old belief was surfacing. I started a dialogue with the belief, and I came to the conclusion that all I needed to do was acknowledge that I was feeling shame, look it in the eye and then move on. At first, I didn't trust that answer. When I did, the shame lost its grip on me, and I was free. When we allow ourselves to look at uncomfortable feelings instead of stuffing them or hiding from them, they process through, and we can get on with being happy and free.

Being human means experiencing a myriad of feelings during this lifetime, and I recognize each emotion as it arises. Emotions are just reactions, and they cause no harm.

Fear to *faith*

324

Today I was thinking about the immense power of the words "I Am." Many of you already use them to declare the truth about yourself by following "I Am" with a quality of God. However, today I realized we can broaden our use of "I Am" to create action we are seeking to experience in our lives.

For example, if we are looking for answers to questions, we can say, "I Am receiving the answers to my questions." Other examples include: "I Am seeing this situation differently," or "I Am deepening my spirituality." There is so much more we can create in our lives by using "I Am" in ways we never considered.

I use the power of "I Am" to set in motion the goodness I am ready to experience in my life.

_____

_____

_____

_____

_____

_____

Fear to *faith*

Within all of us, at the core of our being, is innate goodness. Unfortunately, that goodness gets covered up by guilt, bitterness, resentment and a host of other feelings. Many situations in life can cause the cover up to get pretty thick, especially in regards to how we view ourselves. If we have an expectation that we are to meet the needs of others, but we cannot do so, we can go into some heavy self-judgment and guilt and become blind to that inherent goodness that is within us.

Our healing lies in peeling off the layers of guilt or whatever is covering our light so we can see and embrace our inner goodness that yearns to be revealed and expressed through us. We were not created to be vessels of discordant, self-destructive energy. We were created to hold and express light. Living in our light is the greatest gift we can give to ourselves, our loved ones and the world.

I identify with the eternal goodness that dwells within me; this is the nature of who I am. Knowing that this goodness is stronger than any temporary feeling of guilt or self-criticism frees me to love and accept myself, allowing my light to shine brightly.

326

Someone I was listening to spoke about examining self-defeating beliefs that create unnecessary chaos — or as he called it, fiascos. As this idea sunk into my mind, I started thinking about people I know who have lives where everything always turns out amazingly well without any complications. You might say they have charmed lives.

Then I realized that I want to be one of those people. For a split second I thought that it is too late to shift my life into that frequency, then I laughed at myself and realized it is never too late to create a new energy to be centered in.

So today I am claiming that I live a charmed life, and I can't wait to see how the universe is going to say "yes" to that declaration. What kind of life do you want to affirm for yourself? It is never too late to make the change.

Today is the day I claim the life energy I would like to experience, and Spirit makes it so.

_____

_____

_____

_____

Fear to *faith*

A good friend of mine recommended I watch a series on PBS called "Poldark." Little did she know that the main character represents my favorite hero archetype — the Warrior Poet. The Warrior Poet is a person who is earthy, physically strong, sensitive and who will rebel against societal norms to support social justice and the underdog. When I was contemplating this hero after watching a couple of episodes, I realized that the Warrior Poet is who I strive to be.

Anyone we cast in the role of hero represents the qualities we deeply hold reverent in the core of our being. Take a look at your heroes, and you will see a mirror into your soul.

My heroes reveal the hero that lies within me. I recognize the valor and courage that is at the center of my being, and I give it a voice to express through me and as me.

_____

_____

_____

_____

_____

_____

_____

Fear to *faith*

328

Recently I had a most amazing revelation. During a conversation, the subject of skydiving came up. I have absolutely no desire to skydive, but I was intrigued as the person described what he enjoyed about it: true freedom and the feeling of being unencumbered by anything. I thought to myself, "Why does a person need to jump out of a plane to experience that?" Then I realized that I am a spiritual skydiver. Whenever I complete inner work that liberates me, I symbolically jump out of the plane that holds all of the old beliefs, perceptions and experiences that kept me in a state of lack and limitation. Then I soar into the vast, unlimited potential that is always present in my life, knowing that the invisible presence of Spirit forever supports me. This is true freedom.

I am ready to dive into the universe of possibilities that is before me and leave all that stands in my way behind me. I allow myself to be fully self-expressed and enjoy the unlimited goodness that is mine to have and to share.

_____

_____

_____

_____

Fear to *faith*

Upon arising one New Year's morning, the first thought I had was, "I am going to love myself more this year." At first, I was surprised. Then I remembered that without self-love, any intentions we set or any dreams we want to see realized will be difficult to achieve.

Last year was a deep awakening for me regarding the power of self-love. I came to understand that self-love is not selfish or arrogant; it is necessary for our well-being and allows us to be present and giving to others. Self-love is deeply appreciating the unique person I am, treating myself with compassion and unconditionally loving myself the same way a mother loves her child. To love ourselves in this way allows us to love others more deeply and to have healthy relationships.

As I deepen my love for myself, the divinity within me rises up and fully expresses itself in, as and through me. Life is sweet and fulfilling when I open my heart to myself.

330

When I was watching the opening credits for Stephen Colbert's late night show, I noticed that the name of his band is Stay Human. For some reason, I couldn't stop thinking about those words and what they meant to me. After much thought, I realized how good it is to be human and how often I have assigned flaws and errors to being human.

The heart of humanity is about love, kindness, compassion and caring. Being human is having the power to exercise our free will to make whatever choices we like. Yet choosing unwisely is not inherent to being human; it is a product of our programming, personality and a wide variety of other variables. Today I am seeing the value of being human in a whole new light; after all, God did create us in Its image and likeness.

Being human allows me to express my divinity through love and compassion. I am grateful to be who I am in this incarnation of life.

_____

_____

_____

_____

_____

Fear to *faith*

I must confess, sometimes I get really impatient not knowing how things are going to turn out in various situations, whether it is something going on in my life, in our country or something else. I just want to cut to the chase and know how it all turns out.

I have found that when I get worked up like this, it is time for me to redirect my energy and do something creative. Being creative puts us in the flow of pure, unformed divine energy, allowing us to uniquely express ourselves in whatever form is fulfilling to us. It is our opportunity to bring something wonderful to life and to exercise our innate power to create.

I am an open channel for the divine creative energy of the universe to express through me. It brings me great joy to explore all the different ways I can be creative and bring positive energy to my life and to the world.

332

Something I have seen in myself and others is that we place high expectations on ourselves to be able to quickly heal through challenging life experiences. I know a lot of people who had big traumas in their lives last year, and they feel like there is something wrong with them because they aren't moving forward fast enough. Whenever we experience a great deal of turbulence and change, the mind has to catch up with what has happened. And that takes time.

We need time to process the experience and get used to the changes that have taken place, and there is no set timetable for that. It is important for us to remember that questioning ourselves for what we see as not healing quickly enough only gets in the way of the healing.

I honor the time it takes me to heal from challenging experiences knowing that Spirit's love embraces me and guides me on this healing journey.

Even though I know that our evolution is forever unfolding, sometimes I cannot imagine expanding my consciousness more than I have already. But then I learn something new, and my mind stretches yet again. I think that says a lot about our human potential. If we are open and receptive to inner growth, there is no limit to how far we can be stretched. How is that for being human?

I open my mind to the universe of ideas that allow me to see beyond everything I ever learned. I am so grateful there is more to life than what the world taught me. Thank you, sweet Spirit, for bringing me enlightenment that frees me.

334

I woke up this morning to a feeling of loneliness, so I moved my consciousness to a place of observation in an effort to understand what was going on within me. My mind began by analyzing why I was feeling this way. Many possibilities arose, so the next place my mind went to was how to fix this. As answers were proposed, I had to tell my mind to stop what it was doing. I realized that the solution to dealing with emotions that may be classified as uncomfortable is not by figuring out ways to prevent them from emerging, but instead allowing them to be expressed knowing they will pass. I allowed myself to feel what I was feeling. I am happy to tell you that as soon as I got out of bed, the loneliness quickly gave way to the joy of the beautiful day that was before me.

As I recognize that feelings are transitory, *I allow any emotion that bubbles up to be fully expressed. God gave me the ability to experience all feelings with ease, as I keep myself centered in Its divine energy.*

Fear to *faith*

A dear friend of mine whose wife died a few months ago called me this morning because she can't stop crying. She is questioning if she will be able to go on in her life. After reminding her that this is natural after having been married for 44 years, she felt much better.

This is a reminder to me how poorly educated so many of us are in the area of emotions. Emotions are such an integral part of the human experience, and when we experience challenging emotions, many of us try to run away from them or eliminate them. Then if we are feeling them for what we think is too long, we question our sanity, and we think we are too emotional. Wow! It is so self-destructive for us to think that our natural emotional inclinations are wrong. If we just allow ourselves to feel without judgment or condemnation, we can get through our life experiences so much easier. We all have our own individual processes and rhythms, and we must honor that.

I no longer question my emotions *and the duration of their expression. I have compassion toward myself and all I have experienced, and I allow myself to fully and completely emote for however long it takes to bring balance to my life.*

336

I love the concept of emptying the mind. Even though it is a daunting task, just contemplating the idea activates the release of discordant thoughts from our minds. When we move our awareness to peace and stillness, the serenity it brings to our consciousness naturally loosens our grip on thoughts that disturb us.

In the empty space of my mind, I meet Spirit. Behind all the chatter and distraction, the invisible yet substantial energy of God surrounds me and rejuvenates my soul so I can do this thing called life with energy, enthusiasm and faith.

_____
_____
_____
_____
_____
_____
_____
_____
_____
_____

Fear to *faith*

Every now and then, I think about my human mortality, and if I'm not mindful, my brain will take me to a place of fear. Instead of staying stuck in that feeling, I turn to the deep well of soul wisdom that is within me, and it reminds me of the truth. My soul is eternal and will go onto another expression of life when I am complete here. There is nothing scary about that, for Spirit is my eternal guide no matter where my journey takes me.

My heart is peaceful *knowing that my soul is eternal and everlasting. Spirit is my constant companion wherever my soul may travel.*

Fear to *faith*

338

The great spiritual teacher Ram Dass said we should look at people as though they are trees: Some are bent from the wind, some are flawless, and others have no leaves. In other words, to deepen our spirituality, we must disengage from judging others and see the beauty that each person brings to the world, for they are each products of their experiences. When I first heard this idea, I immediately asked myself why I still get caught up in judging people, and the answer I got is because there are things about myself that I am uncomfortable looking at. Judging another person takes it off of me and puts it on someone else. Looks like I have work to do.

Judging others opens a window for me to look within and heal my relationship with myself. Judgment is just an unmet expectation that prevents me from unconditionally loving myself and others for who they are.

Fear to *faith*

Recently I wrote about examining our consciousness when our desires are not manifesting so we can release any blocks that are preventing our good from demonstrating. However, there is another angle to consider. Sometimes what we think we want is truly not what our soul desires. The surface mind is oftentimes hypnotized into thinking it needs certain things to be happy and fulfilled, but the soul knows what it really wants. If this conflict exists within us, then we will not manifest. There is a lot to consider when we are creating our lives.

As I tune into the depths of my being, I am clear on what I truly desire to have in my life, and the universe brings it into form.

340

A friend and I were talking yesterday, and she said that although she has plenty of material wealth, she is missing love and tenderness. She said that her husband doesn't satisfy her needs, and she was thinking of going outside of her relationship to get them met. She wasn't interested in marriage counseling and had given up on talking to her husband, so I told her that when we look outside of ourselves for qualities that are missing from our life, such as love and kindness, we are not looking in the right place. We need to look within. All the qualities of Spirit dwell within us, and if we are not experiencing them, it is because we are blocking them.

I told my friend that since she is not treating herself with love and tenderness, she is looking for someone to give to her what she is not giving to herself. Our outside world truly is a reflection of our inner world, so if we want to improve the outside, we have to start from within.

The more I give myself love and respect, the more it becomes a reality in my external life. The law of mind is exacting, so I till the soil of my consciousness and plant seeds of love, and I harvest a bounty of God's goodness.

Fear to *faith*

As I was thinking about the power of prayer this morning, it hit me how it is like a sacred ritual for casting universal energy into motion so that our good can come forth into our lives. Ernest Holmes sometimes refers to prayer as the "High Invocation." Prayer is certainly something to take seriously and treat with much reverence. Knowing this is a reminder to me that, before I go into prayer, I must take extra time to sequester my consciousness so that I completely turn away from the effects and conditions of this world and deeply feel the presence of the pure, unformed, invisible substance of Spirit that I call into form through my words.

When we pray we become the artist, crafting the life we desire based on the qualities of life we would like to experience. Praying is more than just taking a few minutes to utter some words of truth; it is entering into a sacred space of deep connection with Spirit and the energy of the universe. So take some time before you pray to acknowledge the grandeur of what you are doing.

I pray with deep respect for the awesome nature of Spirit that answers my prayers with perfection. Knowing that I am a spiritual being living in a spiritual universe, I recognize that there is a power for good in the universe, and I can use it.

Fear to *faith*

During my morning meditation, a couple of stressors in my life rose up into my awareness, grabbed my attention, and I became the stress. My body and mind were held captive, as my inner peace waned. When I realized I could change what was happening within me, I took a big breath of air into my lungs, and as I exhaled, I released the stress I was experiencing.

I never really thought about how engulfing stress can be, how it takes over every part of us and depletes our reserves. I know this is a "fight or flight" response. Our bodies get flooded with adrenaline when stress arises so we can get out of danger. The danger I was experiencing vis-a'-vis stressors in my life was imagined, and I used my imagination to dispel the illusory danger. I reminded myself that I am not the stress I was feeling; I am the peaceful Buddha sitting in the garden.

I use my imagination to create a peaceful consciousness knowing that my spirit is safe and secure for God is my Source and dwells in the center of my being.

Fear to *faith*

Someone once told me that most of our issues in life involve our relationships and interactions with other people. Maybe this explains one of the reasons why we are here in this incarnation: to heal the ruptures and disharmony that exist in the depths of our individual and collective consciousness. Human beings are the perfect catalysts for unearthing our deeply buried inner conflicts, allowing them to quickly rise to the surface. When anyone triggers us, if we can accept that the issue isn't with the person who has caught our attention, but is instead within our own psyche and related to our old wounds, our healing begins. When we take responsibility and do the work to heal our inner disharmony instead of keeping the issue external to us, we are breaking the cycle of energy that leads to disease, hate, violence and war, while also creating a more loving and accepting inner and outer world.

I respond to any conflict *I experience with others as a call to look within and heal any wounds that are coloring my perception. This restores me to a state of divine harmony and love.*

Fear to *faith*

344

As my long day of busy-ness concluded yesterday, and I reached my car to go home, my mind saw an opportunity to start up with its chatter, analysis, problem solving and judgment. I consciously chose not to engage with it by bringing my consciousness to rest in just being. Well, my mind was not going for that, and so began an interesting inner conversation. My mind told me that thinking is a sign of intelligence, and that by rejecting its desire to go into hyper-thought, I am indicating that I must not be intelligent. I was amazed by the hidden belief revealed to me. I told my mind that I was fairly certain my intelligence was intact, and the conversation ended.

There is a greater Intelligence in the universe, and I am a part of It. It expresses Itself in ways that are beyond thought and the human definition of intelligence. I see myself as inlet and outlet for Its brilliance as I relax into the divine flow of my life.

Fear to *faith*

I never noticed how the experience of being surprised contains fear. When something unexpected comes out of nowhere, our primitive brain gets activated, and we go into a state of high alert until we can determine the level of threat and respond appropriately. Pleasurable surprises are easy to recover from because the surprise gives way to joy. Surprises that are not so welcome take a little more time to navigate through.

The first thing I do when challenging surprises appear in my life is remind myself that Spirit is present and guiding me through this experience. The longer I stay in a state of disconnection from Source, the more the fear takes over. Knowing there is something greater within me, guiding me, gives me comfort and allows me to open the door for good to emerge.

Life is full of surprises, and I meet them all with a calm heart and mind. I feel the presence of God's love and support knowing all surprises have the potential of turning into joy.

Fear to *faith*

346

A couple of months ago, I learned a powerful new meditation practice that opened me to a whole new level of consciousness and spirituality. When I learned the practice, I was told that you have to do it twice a day — after arising in the morning and in the evening. Being the good student I am, I have been diligent in following these instructions. However, when my alarm woke me up this morning to meditate, I just couldn't do it. My body was clearly in charge, and it told me it needed to sleep longer. Since I have appointments early this morning, I will not have time to meditate. At first I wondered what would happen to me if I didn't meditate. Would my enlightenment stop? Would my day be out of whack? The answer to both questions is no. I quickly reminded myself that taking a break from routine is incredibly healthy, even if it is a break from our daily spiritual practices.

I listen to the direction of my inner voice for it truly knows what is best for me. When a break in routine is the call of the day, I joyfully follow my heart.

Fear to *faith*

When I was walking through my mom's final illness and transition, I found that one of the greatest challenges was being centered and peaceful in the midst of the intense life and death drama. After much inner turmoil, a day came when everything just clicked, and I felt grounded as I fully surrendered to the experience. I stopped resisting what was unfolding, and I felt at peace. As I reconnected with my spiritual sweet spot, I let go of anxiety, fear and helplessness. I reminded myself that I only have power over my own journey, not anyone else's. I became aware that I had lost myself in the energy of uncertainty and concern, and I needed to return to the sacred sanctuary of my soul.

In times of turmoil and unrest, I connect with the eternal presence of Spirit that is nestled in my heart, and I return to peace.

Fear to *faith*

348

There are many spiritual laws discussed in books and spiritual communities. Two of the most popular are the law of cause and effect and the law of attraction. Today I became aware of another spiritual law I had never heard of that arose through my intuition, and that is the law of motion. This law is activated by our intention.

Yesterday was a challenging day for me. When I came home and began relaxing, I realized I was still sitting in the chaos I experienced during the day. I knew it was up to me to start a shift in feeling. Without forcing anything to happen immediately, I gently set my intention for the restoration of inner peace and balance to manifest, and I released it to Spirit.

By activating the law of motion, my recovery unfolded beautifully and effortlessly.

The law of motion is always there for me to consciously use to create change in my life. My intention is always heard by Spirit, and It moves my life forward, bringing goodness to my path.

_____

_____

_____

_____

Fear to *faith*

One of the most valuable ideas I have ever learned is from Michael Singer's book *The Untethered Soul*. He says that when we experience discomfort that appears to be caused by a situation, rather than trying to change the situation, we look within and change ourselves. I recently caught myself trying to figure out ways to change a situation that was disturbing me, so I turned within and wrote down all the feelings I was experiencing that were making me feel uncomfortable. Next to each feeling listed, I wrote the reason I was experiencing it. When I was finished, I felt like a load had been lifted from me, and I no longer felt the need to fix the situation because I fixed me.

When I feel triggered by situations, I turn within and explore my feelings, and the need for the situation to change in order for me to be at peace disappears.

Fear to *faith*

350

Stephen Hawking advised us to "look up at the stars and not down at your feet." What an amazing reminder! It is so easy to get caught up in our own drama and fixated on whatever might be capturing our attention that we forget that there is a bigger world outside of us. Hawking reminds us to look up and see the vast universe in which we live and recognize that there is so much more going on in this life than our personal drama.

As I turn my gaze upward and see the awesome universe in which I live, I loosen the mental grip of all that has stolen my attention as I relax into Spirit's wondrous creations.

_____

_____

_____

_____

_____

_____

_____

_____

_____

_____

Fear to *faith*

Many of us experience heaviness in our hearts and fear because of what happens in our world. When I recently experienced great fear and uncertainty over world events, I realized I was at a point of choice. I could either stay stuck in uncomfortable energy or I could transmute the fear to faith by reminding myself that there is a Power bigger than the drama that is unfolding in our country. That Power is God.

There is an idea in many spiritual philosophies that says when we recognize the presence of Spirit in all things, we energize It, and It shows up in the physical world in a strong way. The greater number of people who stand in faith will create an opening for Spirit to be revealed as peace, order, love and harmony. Good always triumphs!

As I relax into the truth that God is all there is, I see a shift within myself that allows me to see the good unfolding in the midst of chaos. Good always prevails, and I welcome the positive changes that are now unfolding in the world.

_____

_____

_____

_____

Fear to *faith*

352

I have heard it said that the one thing all beings desire is inner peace. Each of us has our own unique path to obtaining it, but the feeling of peace is common to us all. As I deepen my ability to live in inner peace for longer periods of time, I have noticed that when something happens that takes me out of that peace, I get upset. God knows, I love my peace!

However, I have developed a strategy that allows me to return to peace quickly and easily. First, I identify what is making me feel discordant. Second, I figure out why the circumstance is making me feel discordant. Third, after coming to an understanding of the feelings that have been aroused, I can let go of my attachment to the discord and reinstate my inner peace.

Spirit is the everlasting atmosphere of peace in which I live, move and have my being, and when things happen that disturb me, I easily return to peace by using my tools of awareness.

Fear to *faith*

There is a wonderful Yiddish word, "far-schlepte krenk," and it means a situation that is in our lives that is provoking anxiety and that seems to have no end. I think most of us have experienced this or may be experiencing it right now. If we think we cannot experience peace until a situation such as this is over, we harm ourselves.

While I know it is not easy to extricate ourselves from these types of binding situations, I know that it can be done, and it is healthy for us to do so. The first step is to take charge of our consciousness and allow ourselves to be at peace regardless of the status of the situation. There is only so much we can do when uncomfortable things happen in our lives, and if we have done all we can, we must release it to Spirit, and rest our minds in peace. We have to step out of the story and into the lightness of being.

I know that all situations in life have a beginning and an end, *so I unhook my energy from anything that is causing me stress because it is unresolved. This creates an opening for Spirit to rejuvenate my soul with Its boundless love.*

354

One of my favorite things to teach people is how to become aware of the contrast between the physical sensations we feel when we experience love and fear. Love is expansive and energizing; fear is constricting and draining. Each feeling obviously affects our bodies differently. Love creates health; fear creates disease. Oftentimes when we feel fear, we get caught up and lost in it. However, when we pay attention to the sensations of our bodies, we naturally become intolerant when we feel restricted by fear, which motivates us to shift our consciousness to love. This restores our inner peace and harmony, allowing us to relax into the flow of life.

I am mindful of the physical state of my body at all times, and when I feel constricted or depleted, I raise my consciousness into the feeling of love, and I am able to relax into my divine natural state of being.

Fear to *faith*

In metaphysical philosophies, Source is a common name used for God. I think this word is a powerful reminder to us as to who is actually the giver of our good. In this human incarnation, sometimes we think parents, spouses, jobs or other things are our source, but they are not. While it is human nature to prefer a tangible source, developing faith in the Invisible Presence as our true Source of good takes practice and recognition of Its presence.

As I returned home yesterday from my mom's funeral, Spirit reminded me that although Mom was a great source of good for me in my life, God is my eternal Source, and It never stops providing me with all I need.

As I recognize my oneness with Spirit, *I can see that It gives me an endless supply of good that satisfies all of my needs and then some.*

Fear to *faith*

356

Years ago I heard someone say that the universe is always moving us toward healing, and this idea has stuck with me ever since. We can ignore its call and attempt to run in the opposite direction, but eventually it catches up with us. Spirit has given us an amazing consciousness that, when used properly and mindfully, can heal anything that has caused us to be in a state of disharmony. However, there are times when we need a clue as to what needs to be healed, and our bodies are a great source for that knowledge.

As I walk along my path of releasing my mom, I have been experiencing discomfort in my shoulder and middle back. These afflictions symbolize guilt and the inability to accept all experiences with joy. What a gift to be able to see through my body that which my mind could not access on its own. Now I know what to work on in order to restore harmony and wholeness to my entire beingness.

As I recognize the healing nature of the universe, I listen carefully to its guidance so that my healing path is revealed easily and effortlessly to me.

Ernest Holmes said that the only thing that needs to be healed is the belief that we are separated from Spirit. That means that whenever we feel disconnected, out of sorts or just not feeling well, the first place we should go is consciousness and explore our relationship with God. If there is doubt, distance or distrust, then we have work to do.

We can read so many things about what Spirit is, but none of that is worth anything unless we figure out what Spirit means to us. How do we experience God? In a sunset, in church, in relationships? Deepening our connection with Spirit is vital if we desire a joy-filled life and the ability to walk through any experience with peace and grace. To strengthen our relationship with God, we should spend a little time every day contemplating how we see God in our lives and how we experience It.

As I awaken each day to this beautiful life Spirit has blessed me to live, I connect with my Source and feel Its love circulating throughout my entire beingness.

Fear to *faith*

358

Last week I got really triggered when an expectation I had was not met. It cut deep, and some really primal feelings were unearthed. I did my best to figure out what was going on inside of myself, but I was so stuck in the feelings that I was unable to get the clarity I was seeking. It wasn't until I shared my experience with a friend that things broke open. She astutely pointed out that my unresolved issues with rejection and abandonment had been activated. She hit the core, which allowed me to move into my healing.

Whenever we are going through challenging emotions, if we look underneath the surface to find the cause, which usually has a connection to our childhood experiences, we free ourselves from being stuck in uncomfortable emotions and have the opportunity to heal our ancient emotional wounds.

I see challenging emotions as a gateway to healing my deepest wounds, allowing my wholeness to be restored. I was born to live in peace and harmony, and I welcome Spirit's guidance in releasing all that stands in the way of my good.

The attributes of God give us a wonderful place for our thoughts to organize around so we can restore our balance. Aligning ourselves with that quality of Spirit that we feel is missing in our life ignites a powerful energy that heals. This morning I woke up knowing that my God word for today is "wholeness." With all the shifts and changes I am experiencing, anchoring myself in knowing I am whole no matter what brings me deep peace and inner security.

The spiritual exercise of finding our God word for the day is at once simple and powerful. Once we figure out the quality of Spirit we want to experience, all we need to do is rest in the energy of that word, and it becomes our reality.

All the qualities of Spirit *dwell within me, so I call forth the divine quality that resonates for me to be expressed in my mind, body and soul.*

_____

_____

_____

_____

_____

_____

360

I aspire to keep my energy resting in peace, so when something pulls me out of it, my work is cut out for me. My sister and I own a home that we rent out, and we thought everything was going well with our tenant until our neighbor sent us pictures showing damage the tenant made to our property. She also informed us that he is disturbing the neighborhood. When I heard this, I was immediately filled with rage, and I wanted to do something. I really didn't like how I was reacting and feeling, so it was clear to me it was time for me to open up my spiritual tool box and get to work.

I began with deep breathing exercises to calm myself down, and then I went to prayer. I knew I needed to release the unfolding of this situation to Spirit and trust that all is in divine right order. I felt so much better after I used my spiritual tools. I was able to disconnect from the anger and frustration and replace it with faith and peace, knowing that something bigger is guiding this situation, and all is well.

I am the master of my thoughts and energy, and I use spiritual tools to maintain a peaceful loving atmosphere in my beingness.

Fear to *faith*

The other day I was talking to someone who has spent most of her life reading self-help books and going to workshops, yet she is still stuck in old, self-defeating mental patterns. She can clearly see that her inner critic is in charge of her, but she cannot let it go. I asked her if she ever thought about who she would be without that voice, and she was flummoxed. Her identity is so enmeshed with her inner critic that to silence it is death. It is said in many faith traditions that we have to die to ourselves in order to transform and be free in who we really are as divine expressions of Spirit. We must think like that which we desire to be. If we want to be a butterfly, we cannot continue thinking like a caterpillar.

Today I see myself as a divine expression of Spirit, and all beliefs that do not support that vision easily fall away.

362

Recently, I was experiencing fear around the atrocities that continue to happen in our world. As I sat with my feelings, I realized that fear isn't just about what is before us. When we experience fear, we activate all the pre-existing fear that lurks in the subconscious region of our minds. All of our personal fears and collective fears of humanity come to life, and before you know it, we are paralyzed. The good news is that awareness of this phenomenon restores our power and shrinks our fear to nothing.

Should fear arise within me, it quickly fades when I stay present to God's unyielding ability to bring peace, love and balance to all that is.

Fear to *faith*

In the midst of anything we are walking through, there is always something to be grateful for. Finding the gratitude in life's challenges allows us to move through the challenge more quickly, opens the space for creative solutions to emerge and restores our well-being. If we can discover just one thing to be grateful for in a difficult experience, we are taking the first step in transforming that experience. And besides, being grateful feels so good. Just stating five things you are grateful for not only turns your mood around, it turns your entire life around.

Today, I live in gratitude for all the good present in my life. Living in gratitude brings even more good into my life to be grateful for. I am grateful I am here to see another day. I am grateful for Spirit's love, support and guidance. I am grateful I know that peace and love are stronger than anything else in the world.

364

When I was recently doing some deep inner work to figure out why I was obsessing about something, I realized it traced back to a childhood memory in which my emotional needs were not met. As I was looking at the memory, I couldn't figure out what to do with it. It just sat there. I felt like there was nothing I could do because I couldn't change what happened. No affirmation or self-talk could free me of the pain, so I decided to just put it aside.

Little did I know that this exercise that I thought was futile was actually dissolving the hold this memory had on me. I didn't need to do anything but acknowledge the link between an undesirable thought behavior and its cause, and the healing transpired. I realized that sometimes we don't have to do much to heal an old wound except see the root cause, and the healing begins.

With a courageous heart, *I open myself up to seeing the cause of old wounds, and my healing unfolds with ease.*

Fear to *faith*

Whenever I see turmoil in the world, I know I have to be mindful about not allowing this outer conflict to become inner conflict for me. This morning when I tuned everything out and connected to Spirit, I felt deep peace and the affirmation, "All is well in the sanctuary of my soul" came to mind.

Tending to the peace within during this chapter of our history can be challenging, but it is totally doable. We must take the time to go within, connect to Spirit, and fill ourselves up with peace and love so we can walk through this with strength and ease.

Deep within me is an impenetrable peace that nourishes my soul and gives me the ability to be calm and resilient no matter what is taking place outside of me.

Fear to *faith*

Deep within me is an impenetrable peace

that nourishes my soul and gives me the ability to be calm

and resilient no matter what is taking

place outside of me.

EPILOGUE

"Fear doesn't exist anywhere except in the mind."

— *Dale Carnegie*

The great thing about fear is that we have power over it. It is just a mental attitude we can change through awareness and a little adjustment of our thought. Although it is presently part of the human condition, we don't have to own it, claim it or live under its cruel dictatorship.

While reading this book, I pray you were able to understand that moving from fear to faith is an active process that requires our participation in shifting our thought from darkness to light. Once that is achieved, we can live the life we were meant to live: a life of inner and outer peace and freedom.

It is my belief that we are creations of a Divine Source of energy that is the innate part of who we are. It did not bring us into this life to suffer or to live in fear. We are always at choice, and we can choose faith over fear.

Many blessings to you,

ABOUT THE AUTHOR

Dale Olansky grew up in Studio City, California, where she was raised in a conservative Jewish family. After graduating high school, she moved to Santa Barbara and received a Bachelor of Arts degree in English at the University of California, Santa Barbara. Dale went on to teach English at a business college then became a project manager for a third-party insurance administrator in Carpinteria, California.

Thirsty for a new life, Dale relocated to Palm Desert, California, in 2000, where she was introduced to Religious Science. Following a coworker's advice to attend the services at Dr. Tom Costa's church — Religious Science Church of the Desert — she walked through the sanctuary doors and instantly knew she found her spiritual home and the spiritual teaching she had been looking for her entire life. Even though Dale has great respect for the Jewish traditions and history, her heart and soul are dedicated to Religious Science.

Dale became a licensed Practitioner of Religious Science in 2008 and was promoted to lead practitioner at Center for Spiritual Living Palm Desert in 2012. She enjoys an active practitioner practice, teaches classes on spirituality, leads a weekly Sacred Circle at the Center and is studying be a minister. She currently serves as the vice president of the Board of Trustees of CSLPD.

After working as the administrative manager for a law firm for 12 years, in 2015 Dale took a leap of faith and embarked on a new career as a full-time spiritual mentor. She loves bringing her talents and gifts to the world in an effort to inspire people to see their innate power to live the lives of their dreams. She leads spiritually based workshops, speaks professionally and works with individuals, couples and groups. Her mission in life is to empower and heal people using spiritual tools.

She lives in Palm Desert, California.